The Good Dog Spell Book

About the Author

Gillian Kemp is an internationally acclaimed author of books about magic. Her best-known work, *The Good Spell Book,* topped the official UK book sales chart and was a huge success in the US, Canada, and Australasia. It was translated in Japan and across Europe.

Gillian has first-hand experience of the effectiveness of her spells for she regularly uses them to help family and friends. She has received many letters from her readers to tell her they have used her spells successfully, and to thank her for the accuracy of her predictions.

THE Good Dog SPELL BOOK

GILLIAN KEMP

Chicago, Illinois

The Good Dog Spell Book © 2025 by Gillian Kemp. All rights reserved. No part of this book may be reproduced in any manner whatsoever without written permission from Crossed Crow Books, except in the case of brief quotations embodied in critical articles and reviews.

ISBN: 978-1-959883-98-2
Library of Congress Control Number on file.

Disclaimer: Crossed Crow Books, LLC does not participate in, endorse, or have any authority or responsibility concerning private business transactions between our authors and the public. Any internet references contained in this work were found to be valid during the time of publication, however, the publisher cannot guarantee that a specific reference will continue to be maintained. This book's material is not intended to diagnose, treat, cure, or prevent any disease, disorder, ailment, or any physical or psychological condition. The author, publisher, and its associates shall not be held liable for the reader's choices when approaching this book's material. The views and opinions expressed within this book are those of the author alone and do not necessarily reflect the views and opinions of the publisher.

Published by:
Crossed Crow Books, LLC 6934 N Glenwood Ave, Suite C
Chicago, IL 60626 www.crossedcrowbooks.com

Printed in China.
APO

Other Books by the Author

Celtic Goddesses and Their Spells (Ryland Peters & Small, 2023)
The Celtic Goddess Oracle Deck (CICO Books, 2022)
Tree Magick (CICO Books, 2022)
The Good Spell Book (Little, Brown, 2021)
The Modern Wiccan Box of Spells (CICO Books, 2018)
Mermaids and Dolphins and Magical Creatures of the Sea (CICO Books, 2007)
Faerie Wisdom Oracle (CICO Books, 2003)
The Love Magic Book (Little, Brown, 2003)
Good Witch Bad Witch Spell Box (Bulfinch, 2002)
The Dream Book (Little, Brown, 2001)
The Love Spell Box (Bulfinch, 2000)
The Fortune-Telling Book (Little, Brown, 2000)
The Love Spell Book (Orion Publishing Group, 2003)
Tea, Leaves, Herbs, and Flowers (Element Children's Books, 1998)

Contents

1. Your Dog as Your Best Friend and Familiar from the Big Bad Wolf   1

2. Spells for Love and Romance   17

3. Spells for Happiness and Luck   35

4. Spells for Wealth and Good Fortune   43

5. Spells for Health and Healing   55

6. Dog Divination and Omens   65

7. Know Your Dog by Their Astrological Sign   83

8. What Your Dog Says About You   117

9. Using the Dog Oracle   129

Index   159

Chapter One

Your Dog as Your Best Friend and Familiar from the Big Bad Wolf

Place the word dog in front of a mirror and it reads "god." Is that a coincidence or a fact with deep significance? Indisputably, one's dog is endlessly loving, reliable, protective, and devoted to its owner's (or keeper's) wellbeing. Its loyalty never falters. In every sense, it is a best friend.

Eastern European Romani, living close to nature, have long believed that they can reach God through their dogs. Particularly when out alone with their pets, they expect to experience God's presence. To them, a dog is more than a best friend; it is also a spiritual teacher and even a natural healer of mind, body, and spirit. The Romani's belief, deeply rooted in time, is that their dogs have a sensory link with the divine. Hence, their dogs are loved, treasured, respected, and given responsibilities as a natural part of family and life.

It is, indeed, true: your dog can work miracles for you, like to help you to find the right partner, get the perfect job, or pass an exam. If mentally you engage with your dog's psyche, you link into God, for your dog is a living spirit inside a fur coat able to teach you all about love.

Your dog reflects God because it loves you whether you thank it or not. Your dog is always faithful to you, pleased to see you, and there for you, and doesn't mind what you look like. It never makes you feel undeserving of its unconditional loyalty. You are your dog's God. Think "dog," and your tail-wagging companion will lead you on a journey of self-discovery, making you feel much more in harmony with your dog and life, thereby making you feel more fulfilled and happier. In mediaeval art, the dog symbolizes fidelity. If you are as faithful to your dog as your dog is to you, it will change your life for the better. Your dog is good to you and good for you. Be good to your dog by being your dog's best friend.

The hour in which dusk falls, when light becomes dark, is called "hour between dog and wolf" —an hour of change in which opposites occur. The "hour between dog and wolf" is also "witching hour" for dog-spell-casting. For your own dog-worship, you could make sure that your friend has at least one walk before dusk every day. If not, then you should walk your dog during the hour of opposites. It will know you worship it, and you can both cast spells while walking together.

Your dog's fur and paw-prints possess stored psychic energy drawn from its body and soul. Both are potent ingredients in spells that can work miracles in your life. The dog, more than any other animal that humans have used to serve them, has helped us for the longest time and in many ways.

Dogs are sensitive to the supernatural, as they are to smells and sounds. They instinctively sense approaching thunderstorms, hurricanes, and earthquakes.

Your Dog as Your Best Friend and Familiar from the Big Bad Wolf

Dogs change behavior before an event or catastrophe strikes. Their supernatural skills may be explained by their nose detector, which also grants the ability to identify where a person (living or dead) is buried under rubble, debris, or snow.

Like cats, dogs can miraculously find their way home from long distances because they sense a change in the earth's magnetic field. Cats and dogs are the only animals that have historically lived with freedom inside the home, despite being different creatures to their owners.

Your dog is far more than a pet which teaches you to exercise, comes when called, and guards your home by barking. It is also more than a furry fashion accessory attracting strangers to talk to you. The calming effect your dog has upon you and others can even reduce the risk of heart attack.

The friendship between people and dogs is the oldest and most enduring type. "Man's best friend" as a relationship is thought to date back to the Stone Age, when wolves were never far from cavemen's fires, scrounging scraps of food. Being territorial, wolves regarded a cave fire as theirs. So they kept other wild animals at bay, but wolves joined human hunting—if only as a background presence—to share the spoils. Wolves are actually not aggressive but shy, withdrawn, and able to run tirelessly for miles. Like cavemen, a pack of wolves had a social structure of rank, restraint, order, control, and assistance. In wolf packs, adult wolves assist mother wolves and will even feed pups they are not related to in the pack. Ancient Egyptian monuments display that more than five thousand years ago, the Egyptians had hunting dogs similar to today's greyhound and small terrier types, while in Babylon, the Greeks had mastiff-like dogs for lion hunting. The Phoenicians brought dogs to Britain long before the Romans invaded. By the middle of the eighteenth century, the wolves that once overran the British Isles had all been completely exterminated.

In ancient Egypt, killing a dog carried severe corporal punishment, and cruelty to dogs carried the death penalty. The ancient Egyptians worshipped a jackal-headed god with a human body, called Anubis, who led souls of the dead along the path to the afterlife. Anubis held an ankh, emblem of eternal life, in his right hand.

Because Anubis presided over funerals, he was called "Lord of the mummy wrappings." The Egyptian Greeks combined him with Hermes and gave Anubis the name Hermanubis, shown as a dog-headed god holding a caduceus, symbolic of good conduct and moral balance.

Religions have revered dogs as symbols of divinity and virtue and scorned dogs as symbols of corruption and wickedness. In mediaeval art, a dog is often seen at the feet of women on mediaeval tombs. In Christian symbolism, a sheepdog guards the flocks; it is an allegory of the priest, wearing a dog collar, protecting their flock of people. St. Dominic is represented by a dog carrying a lighted torch. Numerous crusaders are represented with their feet resting on a dog, to show that they were as faithful to God as a dog to its master.

There has always been a sympathetic connection between man and dog that extends to folk remedies. The proverb "take a hair of the dog that bit you" was well-established by 1550. It means "like treats like," and the principle has proved true in medicine and many other areas of life.

Today, more than eight hundred breeds of dog are recognized worldwide. Many have been bred for specific purposes. The modern dog *Canis familiaris* is very different from a wolf.

Yet dogs and wolves belong to the same subgroup of mammals called carnivores. Most dogs are smaller than wolves, but a select few are much larger; they are also varied in color and coat. The behavioral difference

Your Dog as Your Best Friend and Familiar from the Big Bad Wolf

is the result of human domestication that began about ten thousand years ago. Like the wolf, dogs are pack animals that like to hunt as a team and bay to keep the pack as one. As if still in the forest or prairie, they often turn around several times before settling down to sleep to make the ground more comfortable. In the garden or home, they may bury or hide left-over bones or food to retrieve later.

A dog is made from a wolf, whereas a cat has always been a cat. A dog owner's personality is different to a cat owner's personality. They say "a dog is an extension of its owner." Dog owners are sociable: they love fun and dog parks, where dogs and people get together in social groups. The dogs run around in a pack while their owners chit-chat. Dog people are like their dogs: often outdoor types, friendly, relaxed, fun, energetic, lively, outgoing, cuddly, funny, affectionate, and show their feelings perhaps more demonstratively than a "cat person."

Cat owners are generally reserved, evasive, and disappear from friends or home for short periods of time. Some cat people are house-proud; they tend to clean and polish often and, like an extension of their cat, are always washing and preening themselves. The type of cat or dog a person possesses says something about them. Because dogs have been bred for specific skills, the type of dog a person chooses to be their pet is a subconscious sign of their personality. The dog is the person's matching accessory.

We have medical alert dogs to detect illness by smelling human chemical changes, guide dogs for the blind, hearing dogs for the deaf, service dogs for people with disabilities, and therapy dogs for giving friendship and affection. There are cart and sleigh-pulling dogs, police dogs, guard dogs, and rescue dogs. Whether your dog is a pet or a worker, all share bravery, cunning, hunting, and killing instincts with their wolf predecessors.

Cats have always been cats but all dogs, no matter what breed, derived from the wolf, not from jackals, foxes, or any other truly "wild" dog. Although dogs howl like wolves, wolves cannot bark. Someone must have taught the dog that trick. You can teach your dog new tricks to help you in your magical spells, and in return, your dog can teach you new tricks in divining your future.

Have you ever noticed how, when walking your dog, you find money or a special stone or shell that seems to give you a divine message, or confirm the answer to something on your mind? Such occurrences illustrate that your dog puts you in sync with nature. Allow your dog to lead you on a walk and your dog will open your psyche to your life's destiny.

How to Know Your Dog is Your Best Friend and Familiar

Love is the key to your dog being your best friend. It will be your familiar if you treat it the way you would like to be treated if you were a dog. It will respond as your faithful servant when treated with respect; clean bowl, the best food, a warm comfy bed, the ability to go outdoors on demand, and given good varying walks. Treat your dog like a true family member. Talk to your dog explaining what you are up to, where you are going, and what is happening. As you get on with your own chores and pleasures, make sure your dog knows you are considering its comfort and well-being. It will show its love and appreciation by following you from room to room because it wants to be with you. When you are packing for a holiday, it may sit on your suitcase, as if to say, "take me with you." Its body language, actions, and sounds will say they are your familiar.

By tuning into your dog, its super-sensitivity will attune to you. The harmony you naturally share will develop your intuition about yourself, your relationships with other people, your life, and your destiny. Your intuition will deepen over time, blending and bonding you and your dog. Without speaking, your dog teaches you, by gestures and behavior, how to "read" what it wants and needs. For example, your dog pushing its empty food bowl on the floor states a clear request. You and your dog know each other's little ways. Inevitably, you are special to each other.

Speak your problem aloud when you walk your dog. Ask for your problem to be solved overnight. At bedtime, put or call your dog onto your bed. Settle its head on your shoulder and ask for your shared spirit realm to solve your problems while you sleep. As a result, phone calls, texts, emails, and people who enter your life will bring about beneficial changes that support you achieving your desire. Your problem will be resolved.

Dogs have always been loyal to their owners, giving unconditional love and wholehearted total dedication. Your devoted dog can easily join you in casting spells to help you to achieve your life's desires, in your dog's lifetime.

Special Spells to Initiate Your Dog as Your Best Friend

Your dog will not think that you are barking mad if you cast a Sirius dog-star spell. Nor will your dog think that you are barking up the wrong tree when you cast a Dog to Wolf Hour spell at dusk, or a Dog-Days spell on a summer's day. On the contrary, your dog will be enormously pleased that you did, because the spells involve dog-walking and honor your dog's spiritual guardians.

The Good Dog Spell Book

The Romans called the hottest weeks of the summer "dog-days" in the belief that the dog-star Sirius, rising with the Sun, added to the Sun's heat. Sirius is the most brilliant of all the stars, being the fifth closest to the Sun. The dog-days carried the combined heat of the dog-star Sirius and Sun from July 3 to August 11.

Sirius the dog-star rules the dog and wolf. Sirius and your dog will appreciate a Sirius Dog-Star Spell to initiate your dog as your best friend.

A Sirius Dog-Star Spell to Initiate Your Dog as Your Familiar Best Friend, and You Your Dog's Best Friend

You will need:
- 5 star anise pods (alternatively, use five silver coins washed in salt water)
- 2 white or silver candles
- A dog rose (**Rosa canina,** a type of wild rose. Use a garden or store-bought rose if you cannot find a wild rose)
- Your dog's muddy paw-print on a piece of white paper
- A pen
- A mirror
- A photograph of you and your dog
- A photograph frame

Your Dog as Your Best Friend and Familiar from the Big Bad Wolf

With your dog, sit in front of the mirror. Place both candles in front of the mirror. Put the rose between the candles and the photograph in front of the candles. Put the five star anise, or five coins, in a star shape (that will look triangular) around the candles and photograph. Name one candle after you and the other candle after your dog, while you light both candles. Write the word "dog," as well as your dog's name, on the piece of paper that bears your dog's paw-print and place the paper so that it reflects in the mirror. Say:

> *"We call to you Sirius, bright in heaven afar,*
> *To shine starlight on (your dog's name) and me forevermore.*
> *Make special too our loving relationship begun,*
> *Of many dog treats, walks, and lots of doggy fun."*

Place the photograph in the frame and put the piece of paper bearing the word dog and your dog's paw-print in the back of the frame. Snuff the candles out. Bury the star anise or return the coins where you found them. Take your dog out for a good walk to finish your spell.

The framed picture and paw-print is a psychic link that will give you power and energy for good luck when you say hello to the picture and ask for protection before you go outdoors. When you look at the picture indoors, the power of the love you and your dog share will dispel arguments in your home.

A Dog-Days Spell to Initiate Your Dog as Your Familiar and Best Friend

You will need:
- **A yellow, gold, orange, or red candle**

The "dog-days" derived the name from those dates said to be the hottest days of the year. On any (or more than one) day between July 3 and August 11, take your dog for a walk in the countryside or to a park. If you walk with the sun on your left, your shadow will be cast on the ground to your right. Call your dog to run across your shadow and say:

"Dear dog-days, hot bright days, of fun and great delight,
Shine sunlight on (your dog's name) and me, day and night."
They are my familiar and I am their best friend.
May our love last forever and sunshine never end."

Carry on walking and when you get home, finish your spell by lighting the candle and making a fuss of your dog while the flame burns. Snuff the candle out when you feel the time is right.

The Hour Between Dog and Wolf Dusk Spell to Initiate Your Dog as Your Best Friend

The hour in which the sun sets and dusk falls, is traditionally known to be the "hour between dog and wolf." Dusk is the best time to cast your spell to initiate your dog as your familiar and best friend. In the spell ingredients, note that a dog rose is a type of wild rose that is pink, has five heart shaped petals, and flowers in June. A garden or pot-plant rose can be used instead.

You will need:
- A dog rose
- A candle
- A piece of paper
- A pen
- A mirror
- A saucer

Put a rose in a vase of water. Take your dog for a walk at dusk, the dog to wolf hour. Find somewhere to sit with your dog where you can look at the setting sun. Hold your dog's paw or stroke them while you say:

> "Blending with the setting of the sun
> Bind my dog and I as one
> At the dog to wolf hour of dusk
> My dog and I pledge each other trust."

Begin your walk home before it gets dark. When you get home, write the word "dog" on a piece of paper. Light a candle in front of a mirror. Put the rose vase beside the candle, and place the piece of paper in front of the rose to reflect the writing in the mirror.

Make a fuss of your dog while the candle burns. When the time feels right, hold the piece of paper to the flame and put the burning paper in a saucer to extinguish to ash. Blow the candle out. Press the rose when it fades or bury it.

Casting a Sacred Dog Circle for Protection

Take your dog for a country walk or to a park. Throw a ball to your dog east, north, south, and west so that your dog runs in a clockwise circle around you. Say:

*"My dog has cast a magic circle of protection around me,
No evil will approach or enter in, I am guarded."*

Alternatively, if you are spell-casting at home, you may like to cast a protective circle around you and the table at which you are lighting a candle and casting your spell. Throw a dog toy to your dog east, north, south, and west, so that your dog runs in a circle.

Your Dog as Your Best Friend and Familiar from the Big Bad Wolf

Dog Holy Water to Guard and Keep You Safe from Harm

You will need:
- A votive or household candle
- Olive or almond oil
- Lavender oil
- Lemon oil
- A small dish
- Water from your dog's bowl in a small bottle

Pour two teaspoons of olive or almond oil into a small dish. Sprinkle in two drops each of lemon and lavender oil. Rub a little oil into the candle and light the candle. When the flame is established and you can smell the oil's fragrance, say:

> *"Flowers and fruit blend and empower well,*
> *Your potent, magical ingredients in my spell.*
> *Enchanted elixir, that I sprinkle on dog marked grass.*
> *Bless what I have asked for, that it will come to pass."*

Pour the remaining oil into water taken from your dog's bowl and keep the water for a couple of days. Sit with your dog and the candle or, instead, blow the candle out.

Your dog will find where to finish casting your spell when you are walking. Speak what it is you wish for when sprinkling the oil infused water over one spot your dog marks. Go home happy.

Sprinkle drops of dog holy water around your home for its scent to lift the energy. For safeguarding and good luck when you go out, put a dab of the water on your forehead before leaving your home. For your dog's safekeeping when going to the vet or staying away from home, dab your dog's paw with the dog holy water.

Hour Between Dog and Wolf Scrying Divination

At dusk, the hour between dog and wolf, place your dog's water bowl on a table in front of a lit candle. Alternatively, pour the water from your dog's bowl into a glass bowl. Look into the water in the bowl. Scrying is simply gazing and letting your imagination drift into a dreamy state. You may see images in the water or in your mind's eye—that is, your third eye through which you see clairvoyant vision. Images that appear predict places or future events for you. The pictures, which may be people, buildings, locations or items, might also give insight into a present situation that is on your mind or that you are wondering about. Images are often more easily seen in the half-light of dusk than in the full light of day.

Chapter Two
Spells for Love and Romance

To feel a burning desire for someone is emotional power, its intensity directed at someone can produce miracles. You can attract romance or enhance an existing partnership. Creative visualization increases the power of your spell-working. When you cast your spells, create a definite vision in your mind. Think of your future as if it has already materialized in the way that you would like it to. Focus your creative visualization. Giving a word of thanks that your wish has been granted, before your wish manifests in physicals form, also helps your spell to bring your heart's desire.

For a Partner to be Faithful to You

You will need:
- A dog rose (wild rose), garden rose, or a rose bought in a shop (alternatively, five rose petals)
- A postcard or greetings card and envelope
- A stamp
- A photo of you and your dog
- A copy of a photo of the person you are bewitching
- Rose oil
- A pink candle
- A white candle
- A pen
- A dish or saucer to extinguish the burned paper

Using the pen, write on the pink candle the name of the person you are spellbinding. Write your own name on the white candle. Place each candle in a holder and put the photo of you and your dog beside the white candle bearing your name. Put the photo of the one you are spellbinding beside the pink candle bearing their name. Place the rose stem or plant in front of both candles.

Light the white candle that represents you.

Then, light the pink candle representing the other person and imagine light entering that person's mind. Place a thought that you want them to think or feel into their mind by staring for a few minutes, at the flame of the pink candle that represents them. While you look at the flame, flicker, rise, and fall, speak aloud what it is you wish them to think or feel.

Address the envelope and write a warm message on the postcard or greetings card. Dab a little rose oil on your fingers and smear a little oil, as invisibly as possible, on the card. Put the card in the envelope and stick the stamp on the envelope, ready to post, to them.

Burn the photograph of the person in the candle flame of the pink candle. Put the picture in the saucer to extinguish completely to ash.

Sit with the candles burning for as long as you like. Ideally, both the candles should be allowed to burn themselves out.

Scatter the dog rose petals on top of the ash, then bury the ash and dog rose petals. Keep the photograph of you.

To Spellbind a Lover to Give You Unconditional Love

You will need:
- **A candle**
- **A handwritten card or letter from the person you are spellbinding**
- **A book opened at a romantic page, representing the romance you would like**

Put the handwritten card or letter face down on the printed words or picture on the page. Close the book. Ask your dog to sit on the book, wag its tail three times on the book, sniff the book, or walk around the book.

Stroke your dog while you sit with the candle and think of the person. Snuff the candle out and put the book among your personal possessions.

To Spellbind a Lover to be as Naturally Faithful to You as Your Dog

You will need:
- **1 red rose**
- **1 pink rose**
- **1 pink candle**
- **1 red candle**
- **Your lover's signature, or a photograph of your lover (alternatively, write your lover's name)**
- **A pen or dressmaking pin**

Using a pen or dressmaking pin, inscribe your lover's name on the red candle. Inscribe your name on the pink candle.

Put the pink and red candle, in two holders, on top of your lover's signature, photograph, or name handwritten by you. Place the red rose to the right of the candles, and pink rose to the left.

Look at the red candle (representing your lover) and say:

*"While this wax melts, your heart melts for me,
You will feel love now, wherever you may be.
Your heart melts for me with the melting wax."*

Look at the pink candle (representing you) and say:

"I value my self-worth."

Spells for Love and Romance

Look at the red candle (representing your lover) again and say:

> *"(Name of person), may you value me and my*
> *light in your life.*
> *Be as faithful to me as my (dog's name),*
> *Your loyalty will avoid strife."*

Continue to burn the candles through the names written on each. Ideally, you should sit with the candles while they burn out, otherwise, snuff them out. Put the roses in a vase of water and place it beside the signature or photograph.

To Bring a Perfect Partner into Your Life

You will need:
- **A red candle**

On a Friday night, light a red candle. Switch off any electric light in the room. Sit with the candle, looking at it. After a few minutes, say:

> *"Dearest Dog-Star Sirius, it is to you I pray,*
> *Bright star of night, loyally guarding every day,*
> *Please bring to me a most 'Siriusly' loyal person,*
> *In the best possible holy way you can plan.*
> *Thank you, starry Sirius, let your stardust blessing flow,*
> *To me and my dog on the earth below."*

To Bind a Lover to You

You will need:
- **A group of trees**
- **A votive candle (if dog walking in a secluded place)**
- **A rose quartz crystal**

Take your dog for a walk and let your dog lead you to a group of trees. Weave in and out of the trees with your dog. Visualize attracting the one you love to you, while imagining that you are weaving a ribbon in and out of the trees to symbolically bind the trees together. Stand inside the cluster of trees with your dog, to bind the imaginary ribbon ends. Light your votive candle if you have one, and whisper or speak your wish while holding the rose quartz crystal to your heart.

> *"(Name of dog), I bind the one I love to me and to you*
> *For (him/her/them) to love us both and be forever true."*

You may like to sit with your dog and the votive candle before holding the candle to the wind to blow the flame out or snuffing the flame out yourself. Untie the visualized ribbon to leave the trees entwined. Tie the imaginary ribbon ends and continue your walk.

To Keep Your Lover Faithful and as Loving to You as Your Dog

You will need:
- 13-inch length of red cotton string
- A dog brush
- A red candle
- A white, silver, or gold candle
- A pot of compost

Brush your dog, telling them they are your familiar and asking them to help you cast your spell.

Stroke your dog with both candles, then bind the candles together with the red cotton string to bind you and your lover as one. Knot the thread three times while saying:

*"Knot one, my witchcraft is begun,
Knot two, brings my wish true,
Knot three, happy (name of person) and I will always be."*

Press the candles into the compost and light the candles. Put the compost pot in a safe place where the candles will be allowed to burn themselves out rather than be snuffed or blown out.

For the One You Love to Keep Loving You

You will need:
- A rose petal or a small heart-shaped piece of paper
- A dress-making pin
- A red candle in a holder on a plate
- A shed whisker (if available) or fur from your dog's brush
- A large pinch of sea salt
- A red ink pen

In red ink, write the name of the one you love on the rose petal or heart-shaped piece of paper. Pierce the name with the pin and pin the petal to the candle. If you have a shed whisker or fur from your dog's brush, press them into the candle too.

Light the candle. Sprinkle a large pinch of salt into the flame. Say:

"The flame burns with my true love for you,
May your heart burn feelings to always be true."

Sit with the candle while it burns through the petal, heart-shaped paper, whisker, or fur. Allow the candle to burn to a stub or snuff the candle out.

Spells for Love and Romance

To Bring Romance into Your Home

You will need:
- 1 teaspoon of almond oil in a small dish
- **Sandalwood oil (or alternatively, tangerine, clary-sage, ylang-ylang, mint, or geranium oil)**
- **A cotton wool ball from a pharmacy**
- **A pink candle**

Two days before burning the candle, show your dog the cotton wool ball and let them sniff it. Sprinkle a couple of drops of sandalwood, tangerine, clary-sage, ylang-ylang, mint, or geranium oil into the almond oil. For two days, leave the almond oil to absorb the scented oil.

After two days, dab the cotton wool ball in the oil then dab the candle with the cotton wool ball. Burn the candle and stroke your dog for a while. Put the cotton wool behind a radiator so it scents your home when your lover calls to see you.

For a Love to Return

You will need:
- **A pink candle**
- **A stick of rose incense**
- **Rose oil**
- **A rose quartz**
- **Your dog's brush**
- **A plate**

Cast your spell at dusk, the hour between dog and wolf. Light the pink candle and stand the holder it is in on a plate. Light the rose incense stick. Drop a few drops of rose oil into the candle flame.

Stroke your dog with the rose quartz, then, place the rose quartz in front of the candle and incense. Brush your dog's fur with the dog brush, while telling them that the two of you are casting a spell for your lover to return. Take a little fur from the brush and drop it into the candle flame while you say:

"(Name of person), as this fur burns your heart burns for me,
As this fur burns your heart turns and returns to me.
At the hour between dog and wolf."

Enjoy stroking or brushing your dog while the candle burns and then snuff the candle out. The candle stub should be buried or burned.

To Ease a Broken Heart

Because the dusk gradually grows dark, any spell to help you get over a lost love will work more potently when cast at the dusk hour called "hour between dog and wolf." For this spell, you will need to go for a dog walk at dusk.

You will also need:
- **A white candle**
- **A small piece of white paper**
- **A pen with blue ink**
- **Your dog's water bowl**

In the daytime, with your dog beside you, light a white candle. Look into the flame and remember various mannerisms and characteristics, such as speech, dress, lifestyle, and behavior, that you dislike about your ex.

Write the person's name on a piece of paper. Flick water from your dog's water bowl onto the name so the ink runs and blurs. Place the piece of paper in front of the candle.

Look into the candle flame and say:

*"I regain my power
In the wolf to dog hour."*

When the paper is dry, burn it in the candle flame and say again:

*"I regain my power
In the dog to wolf hour."*

Instead, you may prefer to snuff out the candle and finish the spell by carrying the piece of paper with you while taking your dog for a dusk-time walk. While walking, think repeatedly, to the rhythm of your walk, *"I regain my power in the dog to wolf hour."* Bury the piece of paper, preferably at a crossroad, or throw it into a stream, brook, river, or the sea. You will find that you are a much more positive person, who remains superior to destiny, gets on with their life, and meets someone new.

For a Lover to Love You More

You will need:
- **A piece of paper**
- **A pen**
- **A tree with a cleft**

Ask your dog to lick or sniff the piece of paper before writing your lover's name on the paper. Take your dog for a walk to a tree with a cleft. Get your dog to lick or sniff the paper on the reverse side of the writing. Fold the paper to make it small and put the paper in the tree cleft. Stay with the tree for a few moments, asking for the tree's power to make your lover love you more intensely.

Spells for Love and Romance

For an Ex to Stop Pestering You

You will need:
- **A stone**
- **A hollow tree or a dead branch lying on the ground**

Take your dog for a walk in the countryside. Find a stone that attracts your attention when you are walking, or pick a stone up near where your dog momentarily stops. Name that stone after the person that you would like to exit your life. Find a hollow tree or a branch on the ground to put the stone in or tuck the stone under. When placing the stone, simply send a thought to the person that the relationship has ended. Walk away without looking back.

To Win the Heart of the One You Love

You will need:
- **A photograph of your lover, their handwriting, or a sock of theirs (alternatively, write the name of the one you desire on a rose petal or bay leaf)**
- **A votive candle**

When the Moon is waxing, take your dog for a walk in the countryside. Where your dog stops to urinate, light the votive candle and bury the photograph, your lover's handwriting, sock, rose petal, or bay leaf, while saying:

"(Name of person), I speak your name
You will pursue me as a sire follows a dame."

Blow the candle out and continue your walk.

Spells for Love and Romance

For Someone's Love for You to Grow

You will need:
- **An indoor potted rose plant or rose plant growing in your garden**
- **3 cloves of garlic**
- **Dog fur taken from your dog's brush**
- **A pink candle**
- **Your dog's collar**
- **Your dog's lead**

When the Moon is waxing, with your dog at your side, put your dog's lead in a circle around the potted or garden rose. Press three garlic cloves into the compost around the rose plant. Between the garlic cloves, press three pinches of fur taken from your dog's brush into the compost.

Light the candle. Swing your dog's collar three times in a clockwise circle around the candle and rose plant while saying:

"(Name of person), may your love for me forever grow
Call me, arrive, and declare your love so that I know."

Sit with your dog and the candle and visualize the one you have cast your spell upon taking you out on a date. Snuff the candle out and return your dog's collar and lead where they belong.

As the rose grows, love will grow in the heart of the one you have cast your spell upon. The growing garlic will deter rivals.

To Spellbind Your Lover to be Faithful

You will need:
- **A tree your dog sniffs**
- **A flowering bulb, such as hyacinth, daffodil, bluebell, or onion**
- **A 10-inch length of pink ribbon**
- **A trowel**

Follow your dog to a tree it walks to and sniffs. Dig a hole beneath or close to the tree and bury the bulb six inches deep. Gently, not too tightly, tie the ribbon into a bow on a branch of the tree your dog sniffed. While knotting the ribbon and tying the bow, say:

> *"(Name of person), as the tree grows*
> *Your love for me grows.*
> *This knot I tie on the branch of the tree*
> *Draws you closer and binds you to me."*

Find a couple of twigs and place them in the shape of a cross on top of the buried bulbs. Enjoy the rest of your walk with your dog.

Chapter Three

Spells for Happiness and Luck

You make life easier for yourself when you feel happy. Your brain believes what you tell it. Even when you understand the reason why you feel sad, tell yourself that you feel happy or can see a positive side to the situation. Tell yourself every morning, *"I feel happy today."* At the end of a week, look back and you will see you have actually been happier all week. Going for a walk with your dog is always a remedy for the blues. The exercise, air, change of surroundings, and different sounds, will recharge you, especially if you walk where nature thrives, because there you are more in touch with the source of life and absorb its life force, whether you are aware of it or not.

If you have a problem, write it on a small piece of paper and take it with you when you walk your dog. Get your dog to find somewhere to bury the piece of paper with your problem written on it. The problem will disintegrate with the paper.

If there is something you want to happen, write it on a small piece of paper and put the piece of paper inside a hollow tree, or press it into the cleft of a branch. As the tree grows, your wish will be granted and come to fruition.

Spell for Your Dog to Chase Your Problems Away

Using your forefinger, write your problem on your dog's fur. Tell your dog that you want them to shake the problem off when you next go out for a walk. Your obedient dog will walk the problem out of your life. While you are walking, look at a cloud and say:

*"Breeze, blow my problems away,
Clear the air for dog and me today."*

Carry on walking. A few minutes later, look at the cloud you spoke to. You will see the cloud has dispersed. It is a good sign, telling you that the forces of nature are making your problem disappear into thin air, bringing the blue skies of happiness for you.

For A Successful Job Interview

You will need:
- 2 teaspoons of dried rose petals
- A printed interview request
- A white household candle (or a votive candle if outdoors)
- A pen
- Lemon or lavender oil
- A small dish

Put your interview request on the table. Place the candle in a holder on top of the letter, or carry the letter in your pocket when dog-walking if you are casting your spell outdoors with a votive candle.

If you are using a votive candle, draw on the candle a symbol of the job that you want. Alternatively, write the initials of the company you would like to work for. If you are using a household candle, draw a symbol representing the job, or write on the candle the name of the company.

On the top half of the candle, sprinkle a few drops of lemon or lavender oil. Turn the candle upside down and, from the base to midway, scatter a few more drops of oil and rub it into the candle. Put the rose petals in a dish and crush the rose petals with your fingers. Coat the candle with dried rose petals by rolling it in the dish. Place the candle in a holder. If you are using a votive candle instead, light the candle and sprinkle oil and rose petals into the melted wax on top of the votive candle.

Look into the candle flame and say:

> *"Thank you for the job interview that
> I have already succeeded in passing."*

Allow the wick to burn through the inscription. Sit with the flame while it continues to burn, or snuff the candle out. Put your job interview request in a safe place ready for your interview.

To Eliminate a Problem

You will need:
- **A piece of paper**
- **A pen**
- **An unused envelope**
- **A few big pinches of sea or rock salt**
- **A few garlic cloves**
- **Your dog's paw-print**
- **Your dog's water bowl**
- **A hole dug by your dog (alternatively, dig a hole yourself)**

On the piece of paper, write the problem you would like out of your life. Put the piece of paper under your dog's muddy paw to make a paw-print over

the writing. Place the paper in the envelope, then sprinkle into the envelope a few pinches of sea or rock salt and seal the envelope. Leave the envelope under your dog's water bowl for a few days.

Take your dog for a countryside walk to bury the envelope in a hole your dog has dug (perhaps with your help). Put the cloves of garlic on top of the envelope and fill in the hole with your dog's assistance. The salt and garlic will purify the problem and allow it to dissipate from your life.

To Get What You Particularly Desire

You will need:
- **A bag or box of night lights**

Think the word or more that describes what you want, such as *"money or pay rise or promotion"* or *"(person's name), take me on a date."*

Place one night light on the table for every letter in the word or words. Light each night light and speak your request.

Walk or carry your dog three times clockwise, around the candles. Sit with your dog and stroke them. Stay at home until the night-lights extinguish, or blow the flames out.

The Good Dog Spell Book

To Resolve a Problem

You will need:
- **A piece of paper**
- **A paw-print**
- **A pen or pencil**
- **A body of water, such as a river, pond, lake, or the sea, or a bowl of water**
- **Box of matches or a lighter**

Write on the piece of paper the problem that you wish to eliminate. Take your dog for a waterside walk to muddy their paws so that you can put a muddy paw-print on the piece of paper. Fold the paper into the shape of a boat. Put the paper boat in a stream, river, lake, or the sea. Set the paper alight and walk away without looking back.

To Leave a Problem Behind

You will need:
- **Fur from your dog's brush**
- **A drawing pin**
- **A small piece of paper**
- **A dressmaking pin**

By pricking the piece of paper with a pin to spell a word or sentence, write the problem that you want to make go away. Take your dog for a walk to find a wooden post. Crumple the piece of paper up. Pin to the post the piece of paper and some fur taken from your dog's brush. Your problem will disappear.

Spells for Wealth and Good Fortune

We can get what we want by working toward it physically. But we can also get what we want by linking into the spiritual realm, burning candles for light to come into a situation, and stating our intent.

All herbs and plants are governed by specific planets. The planets possess different characteristics that work their power in our favor if we connect to them, using flowers, plants, oils, and herbs in spells. Plants are also governed by the elements of Earth, Air, Fire, and Water. You can harness and use the power given by the four elements by tuning into them as well.

When out with your dog on a windy day, cast a wish to the wind. Face the wind for a wish to come to you, or face against the wind for a problem to be blown away and carried by the wind, out of your life. If you are on a beach, ask the tide to bring in good fortune and take misfortune out to sea.

To Attract Money to You

You will need:
- **Your dog's bowl of water**
- **7 coins**
- **A green, gold, or white candle**

The ideal time to cast this spell is during the waxing moon, either on one of the three nights just before a full moon or three days after a new moon appears as a crescent in the sky.

Fill your dog's bowl with water. After your dog has had a drink of water from the bowl, take the water bowl to use in your spell and give your dog a different water bowl.

With your dog at your side or present in the room, put the bowl of water that your dog drank from beside the candle. Light the candle. Hold the coins in your hands. Tell your dog that the two of you are casting a spell to increase your wealth, which will be of benefit to you and your dog. Shake the seven coins in your hands around your dog's body or get your dog to wag their tail over the coins in your hands. Alternatively, rub the coins one by one over your dog's fur. Toss the seven coins into the water bowl and say:

"Howling wolves and barking dogs thrive
Spirits of wolves and dogs come alive
Increase our wealth seven-fold,
For money to spend and money to hold."

Spells for Wealth and Good Fortune

Stroke your dog while the candle burns and when your dog leaves your side, snuff the candle out and bury the coins in your garden or press the coins into a potted plant that is already growing in your garden or home. Pour water, used in your spell, over the buried coins.

To Grow Your Wealth

You will need:
- **Cress seeds**
- **Seed tray and compost**
- **Water from your dog's bowl**

When the Moon is waxing, growing from new to full, dampen the compost with water from your dog's water-bowl. Press your dog's paw into the compost to make a paw-print. Sprinkle cress seeds into the paw-print while saying:

"Money, thrive from the seeds we've sown.
Wealth, arrive by the time the seeds have grown."

Place the seed tray in sunlight, where the cress will take about one week to grow if you keep the compost moist. Money—or an opportunity to earn it—should arrive by the time the cress is fully grown.

To Attract Wealth

You will need:
- **A green candle in a holder**
- **Fur from your dog's brush**
- **A check or banknote**
- **An unused envelope**
- **A pen**
- **A piece of paper**

Place the check or banknote on a table. Put the candle in a holder on top of the cheque or banknote and light the candle. Brush your dog and remove the fur from the brush. Put the fur in an envelope with the banknote. Sit with the candle and write a list of what you will spend the money on.

Snuff the candle out and put the envelope inside your pillowcase to sleep on it. You may then deposit the check into the bank or use the banknote. Keep the list in your wallet or purse. You will see that money comes to pay for the listed items.

Spells for Wealth and Good Fortune

To Attract Money

Your will need:
- **A 6- or 7-inch strand of gold or green cotton string**
- **A banknote**
- **Fur taken from your dog's brush**
- **A shed dog claw sheath or whisker, if available**

Brush your dog and wrap a banknote around a little bit of dog fur taken from your dog's brush. If you have a dog claw sheath or whisker, put them with the fur. Tie the note to keep it folded. Keep the note in your wallet or purse and do not spend the money for a year, by which time you will see your finances have substantially improved.

To Increase Your Wealth

You will need:
- **Water from your dog's bowl**
- **A small dish**
- **3 well-used coins**
- **2 new coins (if available. If not, use well-used coins)**
- **Your dog's collar**
- **Your dog's lead**
- **A green, gold, or white candle**

When the Moon is growing from new to full, drop three used coins and two new coins into a dish. Cover the coins with water, poured from your dog's drinking bowl. Put the dish of coins in front of a candle on a table. Place your dog's lead in a circle around the coins and candle.

Get your dog to bark, kiss, or give you their paw five times. Or, you can walk or carry your dog around the table five times in a clockwise circle.

With each bark, kiss, paw-handshake, or clockwise walk around the candle and coins, say:

"My dog, (your dog's name), and I attract financial wealth today."

Spells for Wealth and Good Fortune

Sit with your dog, face the candle, and hold your dog's two front paws in your hands while you say:

*"Golden flame (name of dog) and I see.
Abundant wealth, shine on my dog (name of dog) and me.
Turn golden light into money for me,
For financial security, eternally."*

Encircle the flame by swinging your dog's collar five times in a clockwise circle around the candle flame.

Thank your dog for helping you to cast your spell and snuff out the candle. Put the five coins in your purse or wallet separate from spending money. Alternatively, put the coins on a windowsill in the east of your home. To recharge the money, drawing power from the coins, wash the coins in water poured from your dog's bowl just before each month's full moon.

Of course, you will never be without money if you always keep the coins in your purse, wallet, or on the windowsill. But the coins are believed to forever increase your wealth fivefold. Keep the coins in the purse or wallet that you use daily. When you buy a new purse or wallet, put the coins into that new carrier because the lucky coins will bring new wealth to you and your faithful dog.

Baying at the Full Moon for a Needed Money Wish to Come True

You will need:
- **A full moon**
- **A green lawn, dog park, or grass area**
- **A candle**

To attract new money to you and your faithful dog, walk your dog into the garden or for a walk on green grass where you can see the full moon. Sit or stop, look at the full moon, and say:

> *"Full moon, to you my dog (name of dog) and I pray,*
> *For your bountiful blessing upon us this day*
> *And tomorrow when golden daybreak dawns,*
> *Send abundant wealth over these green lawns."*

Go indoors, light a white candle, and sit with your dog. Tell your dog how beautiful they are and how thankful you are for your dog's company, love, guardianship, and appreciation. Snuff the candle out and sleep with your dog on your bed.

Sirius Dog-Star Money Spell

You will need:
- 5 green candles
- A piece of paper
- A pen
- 5 pinches of dried basil
- A saucer

With your dog present, put the five candles in the shape of a five-pointed star. Light the candles. Write on the piece of paper, the amount of money that you need or want. Sprinkle one pinch of basil into each of the five candle flames. Hold the paper to each of the five candle flames. Put the burning paper into the saucer for the paper to burn to ash.

To Win and Avoid Legal Disputes

You will need:
- A votive candle
- Eucalyptus oil
- Ground sea salt or rock salt
- A legal dispute letter received by you

Your dog will send legal people off! Light the candle. When the flame is established, throw three pinches of finely ground salt into the golden flame. Say:

"Salt in the fire, bring my desire..."

Then speak what it is that you want, followed by:

"I will win this legal dispute and keep my good repute."

Sprinkle a few drops of eucalyptus oil into the liquid wax around the flame. Sprinkle a few more drops of oil onto a letter sent to you from the one you wish to win a legal dispute against or to stop a dispute from developing into a legal battle.

Allow the candle to burn or snuff it out. After your dog has stamped the letter with a muddy paw-print, return the letter to its file.

To Keep Your Home Safe or Welcome Your New Dog

You will need:
- **1 teaspoon almond or olive oil**
- **3 drops rosemary oil**
- **3 drops ylang-ylang oil**
- **A small dish**
- **Cotton wool to dab the oil**

Spells for Wealth and Good Fortune

To welcome a dog you have recently chosen to be your pet or for good fortune to come into your home, concoct a little hinge-oil. Pour one teaspoonful of almond oil or olive oil into a small dish, then sprinkle in three drops each of rosemary and ylang-ylang oil. Go to your front door and ask your dog to give you their paw, alternatively, stroke your dog. Dab the cotton wool in the oil, then smear both sides of the door hinges with the hinge-oil while saying:

"Give me your paw as we hinge oil the door,
To welcome in good luck that will preside forevermore.
And for love to prevail in whatever we two do.
In home-sweet-home, which is your home too."

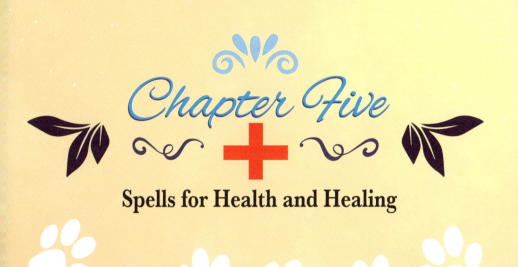

Chapter Five
Spells for Health and Healing

*L*isten to your dog. It intuitively knows whether you are ill or happy. Your dog often knows what is good for you better than you do. When your dog communicates that they want a walk, it could be that your super-sensitive dog sees you are stressed and knows a walk always makes you feel better. After all, dog owners are said to have lower resting heart rates and blood pressure than people who do not own a dog. Simply stroking a dog is believed to lower a person's blood pressure, and walking a dog reduces cholesterol because it is good exercise. If you are ever feeling physically ill or are upset, call your dog to lie down on your bed with you. You can also lie beside your dog when they are on the floor or couch, or can rest your head next to theirs. Tell your dog what is wrong with you. Ask your dog to make you better. Your dog will understand and settle down beside you, and not long after, you will be feeling much better. It's a dog remedy.

To Heal Yourself and Your Dog

You will need:
- **A glass prism**
- **Sunlight**

Lie beside your dog in the garden or the countryside, or lie facing a window or glass door. Hold the prism to your eyes and look through it at trees. You will see an aura of translucent rainbow colors in each tree and around the trees. That energy is the light of the universe. Absorb the energy into yourself. It will heal you and your dog (if you hold your dog), or instead place your hand on your dog and transmit the colors that you see while thinking healing thoughts for your dog and you.

Point the prism at your body and say:

"May the light of the universe fill every cell of my body and being."

Then point the prism at your dog's body and say:

"May the light of the universe fill every cell of my dog's body and being."

To Wash a Negative Out of Your Life

You will need:
- **Almond oil**
- **Lavender, ylang-ylang, or chamomile oil**
- **A small dish**
- **A purple, dark blue, or lilac candle**

With your dog settled close to you, light the candle. Pour two teaspoons of almond oil into a small dish. Sprinkle two drops of either lavender, ylang-ylang, or chamomile oil into the two teaspoons of almond oil. Blend the oil with your fingertips. Using your fingertips, gently rub the oil into your scalp. Sit and absorb the light of the flame for fifteen minutes or half an hour while your scalp absorbs the oil.

Wash your hair in shampoo that you generally use and as the water goes down the plughole, wash the negative situation out of your hair and down the plughole with the shampoo water.

You may like to concoct a final rinse to use after washing your hair to act as a barrier against negative situations possibly approaching you. Sprinkle three drops of lavender, ylang-ylang, or chamomile oil into two pints of water that is warm to the touch. Stir with your hand to blend the oil into the water as best you can, then pour the water over your hair. Wrap your hair in a towel. Dry your hair in your usual way and feel beautiful and protected.

To Put a Thought into Someone's Mind

You will need:
- **A photograph of the person (or their name inscribed on the candle)**
- **A glass prism or a quartz crystal**
- **A white candle or a votive candle if outdoors**

Inscribe the candle with the name of the person you will telepathically communicate with. Take your dog for a walk and find a quiet place to sit. Prop the photograph against a tree. If you are spell-casting indoors, sit with your dog and face the photograph or candle bearing their name. Light the votive candle, or name-bearing candle, in front of the photograph. Hold the prism or quartz close to your mouth and point the glass prism or quartz at the photograph. Speak your words through the prism or quartz to direct your particular thought into that person's mind.

If you do not have a photograph, hold the prism or quartz above the candle, pointing it at the flame. Look through the prism or quartz and speak the particular thought that you wish to enter someone's mind. Snuff the candle or let the wind blow the candle out. If casting the spell indoors, you could leave the prism or quartz on top of the photograph placed flat and face-up, to send frequent thoughts into the mind of the person.

For You to Give Healing to Your Dog

You will need:
- **A votive candle**
- **A rose quartz crystal**

When your canine familiar is relaxing, light a votive candle and carefully hold it in one hand. In your other hand, hold a rose quartz a few inches above your dog's fur. Move the votive candle towards the rose quartz so that light shines into the crystal, pointing at your dog's fur. Say repeatedly:

*"Flame of light, heal my dog with bright new life.
And make my dog feel very well with my loving healing spell."*

If your dog's body has certain areas that are in particular need of healing, hold the rose quartz above those parts of your dog's body. Look at the candle flame, close your eyes, and mentally direct healing power into that part of your dog's body.

Stroke your dog's fur with the rose quartz crystal and when you have finished, give your dog a kiss to make them better. This spell can also be cast outside using sunlight instead of a votive candle.

To Bring Positivity into Your Home

You will need:
- **A candle**
- **Fur from your dog's brush**
- **One of these oils: clary sage, ylang-ylang, eucalyptus, tangerine, rosemary, rosewood, wood marjoram, mastic thyme, frankincense, or cedar**

Stroke your dog with the candle, for the candle to absorb your dog's personal magnetism. Light the candle. Sit with your dog and look at the flame. Sprinkle a few drops of one of the oils into the wax around the candle flame. Then, into the flame itself drop a little fur from your dog's brush and say:

"The negative is burned away.
The positive has returned to stay.
Fur and fragrance brightly burns
In the flame, light and luck it turns."

Sprinkle a few more drops of oil into the melted wax around the candle flame. You will find your mind clears, you feel much brighter, and your confidence lifts. Being happier will make your dog happier. The altered vibration of your home will feel lighter.

For Success in a Job Interview

You will need:
- Your printed interview request
- Rosemary, lemon, orange, mint, ylang-ylang, or juniper oil
- A whole nutmeg
- A green or white candle
- A bowl of water for your feet
- Fur from your dog's brush
- A white envelope

With your dog close by, light the green or white candle. Brush your dog's fur and remove some of the fur from the brush. Sprinkle five drops of oil into a bowl of water that is warm to the touch. Hold your interview request in your left hand and the nutmeg in your right hand. Sit with your feet in the water for ten minutes while thinking:

"I will be successful in my job interview."

Take your feet out of the water and let the air dry them. Blow the candle out. Put the nutmeg and dog fur taken from your dog's brush into an envelope. Put the envelope in your purse or bag to carry to your job interview to remind you of your success.

Absent Healing for Your Dog

Absent healing may help your dog to feel better when separated from you, when they are at the vet's or perhaps you are on vacation.

You will need:
- **A white or blue candle**
- **A small bowl of water**
- **A few drops of rose oil**
- **A handkerchief**

Place the bowl of water in front of the candle. Sprinkle a few drops of rose oil into the water. Light the candle and sit comfortably with your fingertips in the water. Close your eyes for a few moments to compose yourself, then open your eyes and say, three times:

"I send healing to (name), my dog."

Close your eyes again for a while, visualizing your dog well, healthy, and happy, perhaps enjoying a walk with you, or beside you at home. Open your eyes and dry your hands on a clean handkerchief. Keep the handkerchief close to your heart. Snuff the candle out and throw the water away outside.

Chapter Six
Dog Divination and Omens

Dogs are accredited the powers of second sight, able to see ghosts and sense the death of a person they have a relationship with. Dogs win paws-up versus cats when it comes to seeing ghosts.

People "employ" dogs to work in many different ways because dogs possess super-sensitive skills beyond human perception. My own Yorkie dog Rosie's eyes and head followed ghostly swirling mists we both saw moving around a haunted bedroom in a five-hundred-year-old house we stayed in one Halloween party night. As if to protect me, Rosie moved from beside me on the bed and laid on my chest. Just before daybreak, we were both startled to see a skinny, scruffy, long-haired man peering from outside through the window at us. Rosie barked at him. In the morning, I asked my host if the bedroom was haunted. He replied: "The house is riddled with ghosts. My mother had the place exorcised once, but it just made things worse."

Rosie seeing the same ghosts reassured me that the milky white mists and the man were not imaginary. Being led by our dog allows us to tune into its superior natural talents so we understand signs, read omens, and are able to divine on many topics.

For example, when Rosie got old, I didn't want to over-walk her, so I asked, "do you want to walk this way or in that direction?" Following her decisions, I found £40 lying on the other side of a church gate and £10 on a village green. Had someone been around, I would have asked if they had lost anything.

"They Love Me, They Love Me Not" Dog Divination

Using a pen or dress-making pin, inscribe a white candle with your initials. Inscribe the initials of the one you are enquiring about, on a different white candle that came from the same packet, box, or batch. Place each candle in a holder or pot of compost. Light both candles.

If the candle bearing your lover's initial is the first flame to extinguish, they love you not.

They love you if the flame on the candle bearing their initials continues to burn after the flame on the candle bearing your initials burns out.

"How Much Do They Love Me?" Dog Divination

Light a candle. Brush your dog. Take a hair from the brush and burn it in the candle flame. The brighter the flame, the hotter their feelings are for you. If the fur burns brightly, they love you a lot. They have no passion for you if the fur just sizzles.

Dog Divination to Determine Whether an Estranged Lover Will Contact You

Tell your dog that you want them to scratch their left ear to say the word "no" and right ear to say the word "yes." Ask your dog whether you will hear from the person in question. The answer is yes if your dog scratches their right ear before or without scratching their left ear. If your dog scratches their left ear first, the answer is no. If your dog doesn't scratch an ear immediately on command, notice which ear your dog scratches first in its own time, perhaps later in the day.

You may instead prefer to get an answer by asking your dog to wag their tail an odd number of times to answer yes and an even number of times to answer no.

"Yes?" or "No?" Dog Divination

There are several methods you can try to divine by your dog telling you the answer.

1. Put two dog biscuits on the floor in front of you and your dog. Ask your dog a question that requires a yes or no answer. Ask your dog to answer your question by picking up, patting with their paw, or running off with the left-hand biscuit, to answer "no." If your dog picks up, plays or runs off with the biscuit on the right of you, the answer is "yes."

2. Ask your dog a question that requires a yes or no answer. Ask your dog to bark, wag their tail, or tap you with their paw an odd number of times to answer "yes" or an even number of times to answer "no." If your dog is snoring while sleeping, count every dog snore for one minute. An even number answers "no," and an odd number answers "yes."

3. Write a question that can be answered with a "yes" or "no." Put the piece of paper on the floor and place a dog chew or toy on top of the piece of paper. Call your dog into the room. If your dog picks up the chew from the righthand side of the piece of paper, the answer to your question is "yes." The answer is "no" if your dog picks the dog chew up from the lefthand side of the piece of paper.

4. Speak a question aloud to your dog. If your dog moves to the right, the answer is "yes." If your dog moves to the left, the answer is "no."

5. Ask your dog to divine the answer to a question by speaking it aloud to your dog. If your dog runs around in a clockwise circle the answer is "yes." If your dog runs around in a counterclockwise circle, the answer is "no."

6. When your dog is curled up nose-to-tail in a circular shape, walk three times clockwise in a circle around your dog or near it. Your dog will look up at you. The answer is "yes" if your dog looks to the right. The answer is "no" if your dog looks to the left.

"Yes" or "No?" Dog's Bowl Divination

Take three dishes. Pour water from your dog's bowl into two dishes and leave the third empty. Throw a bean into one of the bowls of water. Walk away then return blindfold to the three dishes and dip your hand into one of the dishes. Rearrange the dishes and walk blindfold again, then rearrange the dishes and repeat for a third time. If you dip your hand into the dish with the bean three times, "yes" is the answer. "No" is the answer if you dip your hand into the empty bowl three times. If you dip your hand into the water without the bean three times, the answer is "hope." If you dip your hand into the same dish twice, the answer is "delay" or "uncertainty." If you dip your hand into each bowl once, the answer is "yes." If you dip your hand into the plain water bowl three times, the answer is also "yes."

You can also write the words "yes" and "no" on six equal size pieces of paper, so you have three that say "yes" and three that say "no." Crumple each piece of paper into a tiny ball. Drop them into your dog's empty water bowl. Pour water from another water bowl, that your dog has drank from, into the dry bowl containing the balls of paper. The answer is given in the first piece of paper that rises to the water's surface.

Hour Between Dog and Wolf Dusk Divination

At the beginning of the hour when dusk falls, ask your dog a question that you would like them to divine. Then, with a stick, squeaky toy, or ball, play fetch with your dog, and let them bring it back to you. The divination ends when your dog decides not to return the stick, squeaky toy, or ball.

If your dog fetches the stick, squeaky toy, or ball to you an odd number of times, the answer is "yes." An even number of times your dog fetches the stick, squeaky toy or ball to you answers "no."

Lost and Found Dog Divination

To determine if a borrowed item will be returned, or you will find an object that you have lost, ask your dog to do a little divination for you by using a pair of socks. Write the name of the item on a small piece of paper and put the piece of paper inside one of the socks. Roll both socks up separately and put them in separate places, where your dog will find them in your home. If the sock your dog finds first is the one with the piece of paper inside, the item you have lent or lost will be returned or found by you.

Dog's Ball Divinations

Who will I marry? To find out, throw your dog a ball. Count through the letters of the alphabet until your dog catches the ball in their mouth or the uncaught ball hits the ground. The first name of the one you will marry is said to begin with the initial you were reciting at the moment your dog caught the ball or the ball landed uncaught.

You can also throw your dog their ball to ask who out of people you know will ask you for a date. Call their names as you throw the ball. The name you are calling when your dog catches the ball or it lands uncaught, reveals who. You can also ask:

- *Which of a list of jobs will I have?* **Call out the list.**
- *How many lovers will I have?* **Call out numerical numbers starting with one.**
- *In how many years shall I marry?* **Call out numerical numbers beginning at one.**
- *Will I own my own home?* **Call out "yes" or "no" when throwing the ball.**
- *Will I have a family of my own?* **Call out "yes" or "no" when throwing the ball.**
- *Should I go ahead with my plan?* **Call out "yes" or "no" when throwing the ball.**

Sage Leaf Dog Divination to Dream of Your Spouse-to-Be

Place two sage leaves beneath your dog's bed. Leave the leaves for seven days. On the seventh night, put the sage leaves inside your own pillowcase. Sleep with your dog on your bed. The last words on your lips before going to sleep should be:

*"Show me in my sleep so I can see
Who the (man/woman/person) intended for me will be."*

Or:

*"Reveal in a dream to me
Who my valentine will be."*

Or:

*"Let me in my sleep please see
My (husband/wife/partner) and what their name will be."*

Money Attraction Dog Spell

Put your dog's paw-print under a glass of water in the east of your home or room to attract wealth.

Alternatively, for an increase in wealth, put your dog's paw-print on top of a banknote in the east of your home or room. You may prefer to place the note under an indoor doormat where most people enter your home. Every person who treads on the mat to enter your home is said to increase your wealth.

To Cleanse Your Home of Negative Energy

Get your dog to sniff or walk or catch a toy in every corner of your room or home, or shake your dog's collar in every corner.

Let Sleeping Dogs Lie Spell

When your dog is curled up nose-to-tail, walk around your dog three times in a clockwise circle and make your wish once per time, three times in total.

Sleep Like a Dog on Your Question

Write your question on a small piece of paper and, when your dog is going to sleep for the night, slip the piece of paper under your dog or their bed. Speak the question before going to sleep and you will wake with the answer.

For Career Success

When tree branches cast shadows on the ground, walk with your dog along the shadow branches. Speak your career wishes. Face a tree trunk to ask the tree to make your wish come true.

Dog Spell to Chase a Problem Away

Write your problem on fresh leaf of your choice. Slip the leaf under your dog's collar when you let your dog off the lead in a park or the countryside. When the leaf falls from your dog's collar, your problem will detach from you and nature will work on resolving it.

Dog Spell to Eliminate a Problem

Name a toy after the problem you want to get rid of. Give your dog the toy to rip apart or play with. Once your dog gets their teeth into it, the problem will begin to resolve.

Alternatively, write your problem on a bay leaf or a piece of paper. Dig a hole, throw the leaf or piece of paper into the hole, put uneaten dog food on top, and cover with earth. Your problem will disintegrate.

To Resolve a Problem

Go for a walk in the countryside with your dog. Pick up a big stone and a leaf that your dog stops and sniffs or that otherwise draws their attention. Name the leaf after your problem, or write your problem on the top side of the leaf and the solution on the back. Put the stone on top of the leaf and walk away. As the leaf fades under the pressure of the stone, so too will the problem.

A Wealth, Health, and Happiness Dog Spell

Take a mirror with you when you take your dog for a walk on the night of a full moon. Walk three times in a clockwise circle. Stroke your dog while holding the mirror up to reflect the full moon. Say:

"Bright full moon, my dog and I you bless,
Please grant us health, wealth, love, and happiness."

For a Wish to be Granted

Get your dog to dig a hole under a willow or oak tree. While wishing with your eyes closed, put some dog's fur taken from your dog's brush into the hole. Open your eyes and bury the fur (or ask your dog to bury it).

For a Wish to Come True

Get your dog to smell a bay leaf (but be careful to ensure they don't lick or eat the leaf, as bay leaves are toxic to your dog). Write your wish on the bay leaf. Light a candle and hold the bay leaf in the candle flame and, while the leaf crackles, speak your wish repeatedly until the leaf stops crackling. Bury the leaf.

A Good Health Omen

If a dog licks a newborn baby, it is a sign that the child will quickly heal from any illness incurred throughout their life.

To See a Ghost Superstition

If your dog's eyes and nose seem to be following something around a room that you cannot see, focus your gaze above your dog's head, between its ears. There, you will see the ghost your dog is looking at. The ghost may look like white mist.

Death Omen

It is an omen of death when a dog howls at a door of a room where a sick person lies. The same is said if it howls over the body of its owner.

If a dog howls once or three times, it is said to be alerting you that someone close to your heart has died.

Dog's Dinner Omen

If you drop the utensil you are using to cut or spoon food into your dog's food bowl, expect welcome news or a visitor before dinner time the next day. If you drop a knife, a man will visit you. If you drop a spoon, the visitor will be a woman. Should you drop a fork, expect to be visited by a fool.

A New Friendship Omen

If a dog that you do not know arrives at your door, you will meet a person who will become a good friend.

Good Luck Omen

To see three white dogs together, or even three white dogs in one day, is a sign of good luck. To see a black dog with white spots is also a good luck omen.

It is a sign of protection for a woman or child to see a black dog.

It is an omen of good luck if a dog that you do not know follows you.

Bad Luck Omen

A dog howling at night is said to be an omen of misfortune.

Omen of Ill Luck

It is believed to be a sign of bad luck on its way, if your dog will not follow you.

Funeral Omen

It is an unlucky omen to see a dog cross the path of a funeral procession. It is believed to mean a funeral of someone close will follow.

Wedding Omen

A folklore belief is that a married couple will part, if a dog walks between the couple on their wedding day.

Marriage Omen

Your partner will be faithful to you if, when you take your marriage vows, you have put a little dog fur inside your shoe.

Birth Omen

If a dog howls when a baby is born, the newborn baby will have a difficult life.

Omen of Rain

It is believed to be a prediction of rain when a dog rolls on the ground, floor, eats grass, or scratches itself excessively.

"A Hair of the Dog that Bit You"

"A hair of the dog that bit you" was an already well-established proverb in 1550. In the belief that "like cures like," dog hairs were used in numerous folk remedies, including for whooping cough that sounded like a bark when a dog bit in a fight.

Dog New Home Detection

When you are considering buying a new home, take your dog with you. Notice whether your dog likes the home by wanting to go indoors and shows affection to the current homeowners, or if they dislike the place by wanting to leave and showing a lack of interest in being friendly to the homeowners or person who opens the door on your arrival.

Good Wishes at Your Dog's Favorite Lucky Tree

A tree that your dog marks can be a wish tree; all you need to do is tell the tree that it is your wish tree and share with it your wish. Whenever you walk where the tree is, tell the tree another wish, making your wishing tree special to you and your dog.

Dog Walking Divination Stones

When you are attracted to a stone on the ground, pick it up and look at it either while walking or when you get home. Focus on a question while looking at the markings on the stone. The markings will often suggest images that you see in the stone, which will answer your question.

For a Wish to be Granted

Collect an odd number of stones that attract your attention when walking your dog. Find an undisturbed place to pile the stones in a little upward pointing heap like a cairn, with the last stone put in the center, on top. Without touching the stones, place your hands around the pile. When you can feel the stones emit electrical energy, make your wish. Alternatively, tell the stones a problem and ask the stones to take the problem out of your life. Leave the stones in place and walk away.

Another options is to write your wish on a piece of paper. Get your dog to put their paw-print on the piece of paper, then, let them lick or sniff the piece of paper. Put the piece of paper between two rose petals. Put them in an unused envelope. Fold the envelope to keep the piece of paper between the rose petals in place. Put the folded envelope inside your pillowcase and sleep on it for your wish to come true. Or, you can put the folded envelope under the cushion in your dog's bed. When your wish has been granted, burn or bury the rose petals and paper. If the envelope is getting worse for wear, burn or bury the rose petals and paper and begin your spell again.

For a Wish to Come True

Write your wish on a small piece of paper with your dog witnessing. Wrap a dog's biscuit taken from your dog's bowl in the paper. Ask your dog to dig a hole beneath a rose bush, or dig the hole yourself. If you do not have a rose plant, instead use a different plant you particularly like. Drop the wrapped biscuit into the hole and cover with earth for your dog to walk on (if they will). The contents nourishing the compost will activate forces that make your wish come true.

Spell-Casting When Dog Walking

Find a tranquil place when you are walking your dog. Sit with your dog and visualize your need being answered in the way you would like. Or, you can ask aloud for what you want.

Know Your Dog by Their Astrological Sign

Getting a dog from a dog rescue home or shelter is a good choice because that dog will be eternally grateful to you. You will derive great happiness from watching the perhaps bedraggled and previously flea-bitten dog, in your care, grow a wonderful personality and healthy coat. When bonded, your rescue dog will come when called and will not run away from home, because your dog knows it has your love in your home.

All of us can be matched to a dog of any sign, but understanding the nature of your pet may help you to "think dog" and will perhaps give you a little more insight into your dog's personality traits.

Spells in this chapter are for you and your canine to bind as familiars, so that your dog understands that you are as devoted to them as they are to you. Give your dog true love all the time: your dog is your best friend for life. Appreciate your dog. If ever you meet a romantic match that has the same astrological sign as your dog, be assured that you can handle and adapt to that partner because your dog, your best friend, taught you how.

Your Dog is Ruled by Fire (Aries, Leo, or Sagittarius)

Strong willed and impulsive, your dog likes excitement, plenty of varied activity, and ventures to new pastures. They are very loving and loyal with a strong sense of self, but their impetuous, impulsive, and unpredictable mind can make them accident prone. You can tell a Fire dog by their healthy coat that shines like the sun. Their favored places are sitting at campfires, lying in front of the fireplace at home, or spending time by a window or door where streams of sunlight warm them.

Know Your Dog by Their Astrological Sign

Aries

- **March 21–April 19**
- **Key phrase: I am the leader of the pack.**
- **Stones or collar and lead colors: Diamond, ruby.**

Your devoted Aries best friend, liking to think that they are the leader of the pack and having a deep need to belong, makes your house a home. Your dog loves to be the center of the family, preferably in front of the fire or in the warmest, comfiest armchair. A hot water bottle in your dog's bed or wherever they sleep is Aries dog ecstasy. Should you leave your territorial, protective, and intelligent dog "out in the cold" by not letting them join in, expect to be given the dog equivalent of the cold shoulder to feel what it is like to be put in the doghouse. Your ability to harmonize mentally and physically with your dog makes them unconditionally loyal and affectionately loving to you. But your dog relishes as much fuss as possible from as many different people as possible and will approach strangers in the street. Your Aries dog protects children and family pets and chases rivals off its territory.

Because they like to win, your Aries dog will strive to be the top dog in any skill or competition. Even a clever old Aries dog thrives on learning new tricks because your dog is a winner. Your Aries dog responds to gentle handling and may behave obstinately when driven against their will. With their passion and stamina, your confident dog will relish out-walking you. Your best friend loves to explore.

Bonding Spell for You and Your Aries Dog Best Friend

Your spell will be particularly potent when cast on a Tuesday because Mars rules Tuesday, your dog, and the spell ingredients. By aligning to the planet Mars, you and your most loyal Aries dog can blend to make a best friends pact.

You will need:
- A red votive or household candle
- A dog toy
- A piece of red paper
- A red-inked pen
- A saucer

Cast your spell when you are out for a walk or in your garden, or take your dog for a very good walk, ideally on a Tuesday, and cast your spell when you get home.

Light the red candle. Give your dog a toy and tell them that they are very special to you. Write your name in red ink on a piece of red paper, then write your dog's name on top of your name to entwine both names as one.

Switch off any electric light and sit with your dog in the candlelight. While you are stroking your dog, look at your dog and say:

*"I'll be as faithful to you (your dog's name) as you are to me
We will be best friends in loving harmony."*

Know Your Dog by Their Astrological Sign

*You are my dog. I will always look after you.
Because I love you, to you I will always be true."*

Burn the piece of paper in the flame and put the burning paper in the saucer. Bury the ash or cast it to the wind. Sit with your dog and the candle until you feel ready to blow the candle out. At bedtime, make sure your dog is comfortable on your bed or in their bed.

Leo

- **July 23–August 22**
- **Key phrase: I create happiness and fun.**
- **Stones or collar and lead colors: Amber, topaz, sardonyx; gold, orange, yellow.**

Your extraordinarily faithful Leo dog, with a coat that shines like the sun, needs to feel valued and loves rewards. With other pets, your dog will be the dominant, proud leader and will regard children as part of their litter and kingdom it is their duty to protect. If you get lost when walking, your warm hearted, confident dog will more than likely find the right path for the pair of you to find home.

Like a dog with a bone, your dogmatic Leo dog will rarely give up on anything it gets its teeth into. Being sensitive and easily hurt, betrayal will be expressed by drama to become the center of attention. They take commands well, dislike isolation, and love freedom.

A Leo dog needs firm leadership without crushing their spirit. To blossom, they need plenty of love and delicate understanding if they are not to become too full of their instinct to rule. Show your dog the right way and do not dwell on their mishaps because if you dampen their bright spirit, your magnanimous and self-confident Leo dog may not try again. Instead, let your dog's warm personality shine brightly.

Your dog is a leader rather than a follower with a flair for mounting the throne at dog shows or in competitions. Your Leo dog's bright, affectionate, cheerful presence will be indispensable brightness in your life.

Bonding Spell for You and Your Leo Dog Best Friend

Your dog is ruled by the Sun, which also rules Sunday, so your spell will be aligned to your dog more potently when cast on a Sunday. Sunday walks should be special dog-walking days.

You will need:
- **A yellow votive or household candle**
- **Sandalwood oil**
- **A glass prism or rose quartz**
- **Fur from your dog's brush**
- **A little hair from your own hairbrush or comb**

Smear the candle with a few drops of sandalwood oil. Light the candle. Hold the crystal or rose quartz to your dog's heart and say:

> *"Light of the sun*
> *Shine on my Leo dog and me,*
> *To share as one,*
> *A life of fondness and very much fun.*
> *To each other, may we always be,*
> *Faithful, kind, and loving, eternally."*

Hold the quartz to your own heart and repeat the incantation.

Place the rose quartz next to your dog or in front of the candle. Pour three drops of oil into the melted wax around the candle flame.

Burn three strands of dog fur and three strands of your own hair in the candle flame. Stroke and talk to your dog until you are ready to snuff the candle out.

⭐ Sagittarius ⭐

- **November 22–December 21**
- **Key phrase: I think and feel deeply.**
- **Stones or collar and lead colors: Turquoise; blue-green.**

Your Sagittarian dog is not one for being shut indoors because they love freedom and exploration. You can depend upon your dog's good behavior if you take them with you wherever you can, and it is best to, because they will be boisterously wild and restless if kept from the great outdoors. Your adventure and travel-loving Sagittarian dog learns easily and is great fun, physically strong, and well-built. Whatever their size, they have a big presence and are more likely to use hard-to-ignore body language than barking to tell you something or get what they want.

Liking to do things their way, your Sagittarian dog will have amusing, unique behavior and idiosyncrasies that develop from constantly finding new ways to express their lovely personality. Your dog is intuitive and will easily pick up on how you are feeling. They will know by the look in your eyes whether you mean yes or no to something they may want to do. Your dog will prove to be your best friend, and no challenge will be too great when it comes to protecting you and your home. Dog training and agility competitions will be fun for your sociable dog, but they are unlikely to like taking part in dog shows. Your fire sign dog will love swimming, playing ball, fetching sticks, and generally being athletic.

Know Your Dog by Their Astrological Sign

Bonding Spell for You and Your Sagittarius Best Friend

Thursday is a good dog-walking day and a good day to cast your spell because Jupiter rules that day, your dog, and the spell ingredients.

You will need:
- **A blue-green votive or household candle**
- **Five cloves**
- **Five oak leaves or acorns**

Begin your spell by taking your dog for a walk to find five acorns or oak leaves. Thank the tree that grew them, enjoy the rest of your walk, and go home with the acorns or oak leaves. Brush and make a fuss of your dog so they become lively. To imbue the candle with your dog's personal magnetic energy, stroke your dog with the candle, then touch your dog's nose, tail, ears, and paws with the candle. Press five cloves into the wax around the candle, then, put the five acorns or oak leaves in a circle around the candle holder. Light the candle and say:

> *"Bright rays of love-light burning in the candle glow,*
> *Warmly watch (dog's name) and my love fondly grow,*
> *Best friends bound by long-lasting, loving faithfulness,*
> *I honor and pledge no dog-walking time wastefulness."*

Sit and stroke your dog, give them a treat or a toy, or play with your dog by the candlelight.

Your Dog is Ruled by Earth (Taurus, Virgo, or Capricorn)

Your dog is resistant to change in your home life. They love food, your bed or theirs, and your armchair, and an item of your clothing to snuggle up to for earthly comforts. Your dog demands to be stroked and touched. Non-action leads them to loneliness. Your dog will show you warm appreciation when they feel mud, grass, countryside, a garden, or park beneath their paws. They will display a profound sense of duty to you.

Taurus

- April 20–May 20
- **Key phrase: I have you and you have me.**
- **Stones or collar and lead color: Emerald; green.**

Your mentally and physically beautiful Taurus dog has a particularly attractive face and sharp-hearing ears to match their magnetic personality. Your dog wolfs their food straight down their throat, as if they have never eaten and may never eat again. Stubborn, they are not easily convinced to get into the car after a walk or to visit the vet, or swallow even a well-disguised pill.

Your dog is a methodical, rather than quick, learner, but what is taught is retained forever. Kind coaxing, not reprimanding, is the key to training your especially faithful dog, who is also a very good sire or dam because they are good at breeding and nurturing. You can be sure your tightly clinging dog will never misplace their affection for you. Having a deep insight into people's characters, your self-reliant dog would rather patiently wait guarding home for a few hours than be left with extended family, friends, or, horror of all horrors, in a kennel when you travel. As a good worker, your dog likes to have a purpose in life that revolves around you. They are deeply sympathetic with other dogs and pets, which will manifest as love, a great sense of humor, and vocal appreciation that must never be restricted by a tight collar. Your dog is more likely to be a country-dog rather than a city-dog who needs a walk wherever you live and within reason, whatever the weather. Your dog's happiest moments are with you.

Bonding Spell for You and Your Taurus Best Friend

A good dog-walking and spell-casting day is Friday because it is ruled by the love planet, Venus, which also governs your dog and the spell ingredients.

You will need:
- **A green candle**
- **Rose or vanilla oil**
- **Salt**
- **One of your scarves or sweaters**

Wear a scarf or sweater when you take your dog for a good walk, ideally on a Friday as it would align your spell well. When you return, put the warm, comfortable knit or scarf you wore on the walk beside, under, or over your dog.

Sprinkle a few drops of rose or vanilla oil onto the candle. Smooth the oil in from the top to midway. Flip the candle over and smear oil from the base to midway. Light the candle, and stroke your dog by running your hand over the scarf or sweater.

Kiss your dog's head and two front paws. Sprinkle the salt into the candle flame and say:

> *"Amber flame with flickering hue,*
> *Warm the love (your dog's name) knows is true.*
> *I'll walk my dog whatever the weather,*
> *For (your dog's name) and I to mingle together.*
> *For (your dog's name) to experience cruelty, never,*
> *Each other's best friend forever and ever."*

Virgo

- **August 23–September 22**
- **Key phrase: I am your devoted servant.**
- **Stones or collar and lead colors: Chrysolite, peridot; pink, yellow.**

You have a physically neat and attractive, well-behaved friend for life who is cool and reserved to other people but warm and loving to you. Your devoted, sensitive Virgo dog understands you so intuitively that they will help you

realize your full potential and become far more complete than you would be without their help. Quick to learn, they are easily trained but nervous about being told off and loud noises, such as thunder and traffic. Your dog is finicky about food and will probably not eat when someone or something has upset them. They like their bed to be clean and will hide bones and toys rather than leave them strewn across the floor. As they like cleanliness, they will not mind being bathed and enjoy being groomed.

Your Virgo dog is very disciplined, loves home but not confinement, and likes meals and walks at the same time every day. A great protector who loves work and aims to please, your dog would be a particularly good service dog, instinctively efficient at looking after a person with disabilities. Your dog is a pack leader who rules the roost with other pets sharing your home. Not overly physical, your quick-thinking, analytical, highly dependable, and mentally stable Virgo dog deserves lots of physical and verbal reassurance of your love in return for being so wonderful.

Bonding Spell for You and Your Virgo Dog Best Friend

Wednesday is a good dog-walking and spell-casting day because it is ruled by Mercury, which governs your dog and the spell ingredients.

You will need:
- **A silver candle**
- **Bergamot or lavender oil**

Begin your spell by taking your dog for a walk to a hilltop or woods. Otherwise go to an open space. Light the votive candle. Look up to the sky and say:

> *"Dear God, (name of your dog) sends their love*
> *And I send you my love too.*
> *Please bless us both with love from Heaven above*
> *Yours faithfully, we two."*

Go home. Roll the silver candle on your dog's fur. Smear bergamot or lavender oil on to the candle from the top to midway, then flip the candle over and smear oil from the base to midway. Light the candle.

When the flame is established, drop a few drops of lavender oil into the liquid wax around the flame and say:

> *"This bright burning flame sanctifies*
> *My dog and I together as one.*
> *Whether under moonlit, midnight starry skies,*
> *Or mad dog and Englishmen's mid-day sun.*
> *We'll always be together bound in everlasting love,*
> *As well as when I'm on earth below and my dog's in Heaven above."*

Make a fuss of your dog while you sit with the candle before blowing or snuffing the candle out.

Know Your Dog by Their Astrological Sign

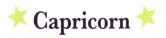
Capricorn

- **December 22–January 19**
- **Key phrase: I am the leader of the pack.**
- **Stones or collar and lead colors: Garnet, ruby; red, black.**

Everyone will love your Capricorn dog, who takes an active interest in everyone and everything. Being competitive and highly ambitious, they are ideal working and competition dogs. Your loving, intelligent, and tactile dog will devise a way to get more affection from you than other pets they may be jealous of. Trustworthy, they look after children well and are heroes in emergencies.

Your Capricorn dog takes life seriously and may not play as much as others during puppyhood but, great in stamina, will usually have a longer life than most of its breed. If yours is a well-cared-for mongrel, it may well live the longest of all.

It is unlikely that your food-liking Capricorn is a fussy eater. Inquisitive and physical, it likes travel and adventures, especially in hills and mountains alone with you because they have a one-on-one personality, deeply appreciating an interesting, active, and mentally stimulating owner. Too much time indoors will make your emotionally sensitive Capricorn dog sad.

Your quick-thinking Capricorn dog will be easy to train. You won't need to teach your dog anything if it knows you love it. When they know they are loved, your Capricorn dog will be obedient and good because it will want to please you.

Bonding Spell for You and Your Capricorn Dog Best Friend

Saturn rules your dog, Saturday, and spell ingredients, making Saturday a particularly powerful day for casting your dog-spell.

You will need:
- **A green or blue candle**
- **A small empty compost pot and bag to carry it in**
- **A trowel or spoon to remove compost**
- **Sprigs of holly or stems of** *Mimosa pudica*

Take your dog for a walk somewhere that your dog can feel the earth beneath their paws.

Dig out some of the earth where your dog has stood, walked, or run. Put the earth in the compost pot and take it home after enjoying the rest of your walk.

When you return, push the candle into the earth. Place a bunch of holly or *Mimosa* in a vase beside the candle, then light the candle and say:

"Candle flame, I ask you to bless
(Your dog's name) to be filled with happiness
Shine your light on all that we do
For us to be companions our whole lives through."

Stroke and play with your dog or give your dog a massage and allow the candle to burn through to a stub. You might like to press one or two of the *Mimosa*

Know Your Dog by Their Astrological Sign

stems by putting them between tissues inside the back of a heavy book, leaving them for a month. When dried, put the flowers in the pages of a favorite book. Keep the water in the vase topped up until the holly or *Mimosa,* sacred to your Capricorn dog, fades.

Your Dog is Ruled by Air (Gemini, Libra, or Aquarius)

Idealistic and easily perturbed by disturbing sounds, smells, and tastes, these dogs flit from one toy or person to the next, even though their loyalty ultimately lies with you. They will probably scatter their toys all around your home. Sensitive to people's thoughts and atmospheres, they like having the freedom to wander from indoors to outside. Air dogs are likely to love having their head out the car window to smell the air and feel it running through their fur.

 Gemini

- May 21–June 21
- **Key phrase: I can easily communicate with you.**
- **Stones or collar and lead colors: Agate, turquoise, emerald; yellow, turquoise.**

Your quick-witted Gemini dog will talk to you and understand every word you say to them. Loveable and fun loving with a great sense of humor, your

Gemini dog will behave and look puppy-like, no matter their age. Brilliantly clever and logical, they are easily housetrained. Thriving on mental stimulation, they quickly learn and invent new tricks. Your dog might teach you a few tricks to accommodate its needs, such as turning a cushion flat on the sofa to make the sofa more comfortable. Communication is vital to your Gemini dog, and you will both have new friends because it will introduce you to owners of dogs it meets.

Your Gemini dog loves playing with children. Mentally alert, they run with mercurial speed and are good in agility competitions and at gaining recognition. Loving to be spoken to all the time, they'll talk in different barks and noises and convey body language messages to you. Gemini dogs will learn the names of different items, such as "ball" and "squeaky toy" and fetch them for you when asked. Your Gemini dog will ask strangers to stroke them or pay them interest.

Disliking monotony and needing a twin, your Gemini dog will want to be with you all the time and will feel pained when separated from you. Left snuggled up in a sweater of yours is the next best thing. You have a best friend for life in a Gemini dog and will meet interesting acquaintances and go to unusual places through them. Your Gemini dog will tune into you too, and you will share a good rapport.

Know Your Dog by Their Astrological Sign

Bonding Spell for You and Your Gemini Dog Best Friend

Wednesday is ruled by Mercury, which rules your dog and the spell ingredients, which makes it a good dog-walking or spell-casting day.

You will need:
- A yellow votive candle or household candle
- A mirror
- Lavender oil
- A few pinches of finely ground salt
- Almond oil
- Your dog's brush

Take your dog for a good walk for a change of air, and cast your spell with a votive candle if you would like to. Light the candle. Sit in front of a mirror or hold a mirror to your face and your dog's face so that your dog can see both of you in the mirror. Say to your dog:

> *"The reflection in the mirror clearly shows,*
> *At the end of your Gemini furry doggy nose,*
> *That I reflect you and you reflect me,*
> *So I promise to you to always be,*
> *As faithful to you as you are to me,*
> *I'll be loyal, true, and loving to you,*
> *And your best friend your whole life through."*

The Good Dog Spell Book

Dab the four corners of the mirror with lavender oil. Place the mirror face up in front of the candle. Sprinkle salt into the flame then add a few drops of lavender oil into the melted wax around the flame.

Drop a little almond oil into the palms of your hands and stroke your dog's coat. Brush your dog to work the almond oil through and their coat will shine. Blow or snuff the candle out when you are ready and after your dog is thoroughly contented.

 Libra

- **September 23–October 23**
- **Key phrase: We need fair play.**
- **Stones or collar and lead colors: Opal; blue, pink.**

Your lovely, loyal Libra dog is deeply intuitive and understands your human nature. They may dislike certain people you meet because they can understand and see through the motives of others. Follow your dog's intuition and you will find yourself among genuine intellectual companions in interesting social circles.

A harmonious relationship with you and approval of your friends is vital to your dog's need for sympathetic balance and justice for you in every situation. Your dog will diffuse arguments by attracting your attention as well as asking you to play. Interested, friendly, and tolerant to other animals, your dog may allow another family pet to be top dog. Your dog will easily grasp house training and will quickly and eagerly learn to be an unflustered, competent, working or caring dog. Independent, they like their quiet

Know Your Dog by Their Astrological Sign

moments and will find somewhere for a little solitude, such as behind a sofa or under a desk. They might sleep at the end of the bed, but in the morning, you will wake to their head on your pillow.

Your extremely good-looking Libra dog will strive to make a favorable impression in your life. A happy dog makes a happy, harmonious home and life when you genuinely understand, appreciate, and love your dog. Their sense of independence will deepen if you ignore their importance. Your Libra dog is intensely devoted to you.

Bonding Spell for You and Your Libra Dog Best Friend

Friday is a good spell-casting and dog-walking day because Venus rules your dog, Friday, and the spell ingredients.

You will need:
- **A pink candle**
- **A fresh or dried apricot**
- **A dress-making pin**
- **Thyme oil**
- **Fur from your dog's brush**
- **Your dog's collar and lead**

Put your dog's collar in a circle around the candle holder on the table. Put your dog's lead in a larger circle around the collar.

Sprinkle a few drops of thyme oil on to the candle, and smooth the oil into the candle from the top to midway and from the base to midway. Light the candle. Brush and talk to your dog, then, take a few strands of fur from the brush and burn the fur in the candle flame while you say:

"Bless my dog with a long and happy, healthy life,
Carefree from cruelty, worries, and strife.
I will love my dog until the end of time.
Likely for them to be sooner than is mine.
I know I will miss (name of dog) beside me when they return to you fine.
So please grant (name of dog) a lovely long, healthy life, dear spirit divine."

Use the pin to prick your name and your dog's name onto the apricot, then eat the apricot, offering a piece to your dog. If your dog doesn't like it, just wash and eat the piece of apricot yourself. Allow the candle to burn while you give your dog a good stroke.

★ Aquarius ★

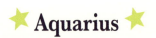

- **January 20–February 19**
- **Key phrase: I love everybody and everyone loves me.**
- **Stones or collar and lead colors: Amethyst; purple, blue, lilac.**

Your Aquarius dog's love for you is so sincere and deep, your dog will make your life more fun, intriguing, and complete. They are a good judges of character and are likely to keep out of the way of people that they dislike.

Know Your Dog by Their Astrological Sign

Being sensitive to your love, your dog will notice your slightest sadness, stress, or inadvertent inattention. Yours is a very intuitive, home-and-comfort-loving dog with an imaginative mind and active spirit of adventure. Your dog is simple to train if the key is love.

Your misunderstanding or anger will bring out your dog's obstinate, self-willed nature. They are unlikely to need strict discipline. From memory, your super-clever dog will always recognize people, places, sounds, and scents it finds in interesting locations where you take it to run free. This is an easily bored dog who will not be tied down or restricted to routine. Easy-going and very affectionate, they cannot bear loneliness. Liking company, your dog will get on well with other family pets and is more likely to be one of the pack than the leader.

Because your dog possesses a lovely personality, it has a great talent for being liked and well-known by people and dogs in the dog park. Some dogs might think it's the sexiest dog it has ever met.

Accepting you as you are, your dog's aim in life is to do all that it can to help you. Too close to you will never be too close for comfort, because your dog's love has no boundaries.

Bonding Spell for You and Your Aquarius Dog Best Friend

Your dog is ruled by Uranus, which also rules Saturday and the spell ingredients. Saturday is a good dog-walking and spell-casting day.

You will need:
- **A blue candle**
- **Growing ivy that you have picked outdoors, or a small potted ivy plant**

Begin with a walk to pick a few strands of ivy from a tree and take the ivy home with you.

At home, arrange the ivy on the table, in a circle around the candle holder, or put the ivy plant in front of the candle. Light the candle and say:

"I will cling to (your dog's name) and (your dog's name) will cling to me,
Like ivy clinging to the trunk of a tree.
Because they are faithful, obedient they will be,
They simply want to show their love for me,
My dog (your dog's name) will never go astray.
For I will care for them in every possible way."

Sit with the candle while it burns. Keep the ivy in a vase of water. Alternatively, press the ivy into compost in a pot or outside in soil for the ivy to continue growing. If you bought potted ivy, keep it indoors or plant it out.

Know Your Dog by Their Astrological Sign

Your Dog is Ruled by Water (Pisces, Cancer, or Scorpio)

Your dog knows when someone approves or disapproves of them and is particularly sensitive to criticism. Your dog has a natural instinct for what you and the other people around them need. They can easily, and lovably, get their way by playing on people's emotions. Your dog has a sense of humor and likes happy, but not dull or loud, people. Highly emotional, your dog has difficulty detaching you from their own deep feelings. They are incredibly loyal: in their mind, you and your dog are one. You are their soul mate. They like water and are good swimmers.

Pisces

- February 19–March 20
- **Key phrase: I know you are the leader of the pack.**
- **Stones or collar and lead colors: Pearl, aquamarine; cream, blue, green.**

Your naturally patient, obedient, and very home-loving Pisces dog has a deep appreciation for kindness and shrinks from harsh words. They enjoy being indulged in comfort and conversation at home. Being observant, perceptive, and intelligent, they are quick to learn. Your dog is unlikely to forget where it buried a chew or which cupboard stores its food. As a puppy or when new to the household, they may be timid and need training by

107

gentleness and reward. Seashores and riversides, especially where they can splash in water, are favorite paths for walks. Your dog will charm all people and dogs it meets, and one or two may charm you.

For security, your dog is likely to prefer to sleep with you or under or behind something. Rather fussy with food, your dog is not usually the type to swipe food from your plate or raid a bin. But it is unlikely your docile dog will allow you or another dog to succeed in taking their toy or chew; their agility and brain means they usually win paws-up.

Preferring freedom and daily variety rather than complying with strict conformity, your intuitive dog will never stop surprising you with new ways to communicate with you through barks and body language. Your loveable, non-aggressive, adaptable dog will bring out the best and happiest version of you. They understand your inner sentiments and will always be exceedingly kind and loyal to you.

Bonding Spell for You and Your Pisces Dog Best Friend

Your dog is ruled by Neptune, which also governs Thursday and the spell ingredients. Thursday is a good dog-walking and spell-casting day.

You will need:
- **1 teaspoon of grated nutmeg**
- **Water from your dog's bowl**
- **A cream-colored candle**

Know Your Dog by Their Astrological Sign

- **Ylang-ylang oil**
- **Ink pen**
- **Small piece of paper**
- **A dish or saucer**
- **Ground nutmeg**

Begin your spell by taking your dog for a good walk.

When you arrive home, light the candle. Using your forefinger write your name and your dog's name in cursive writing on their fur to join your name to your dog's.

Write both your names joined together on the piece of paper. Flick water from your dog's bowl on the paper to smudge the ink. Fold the piece of paper in half, ink side inwards, to further smudge the ink.

Drop a few pinches of nutmeg into the burning candle flame and say:

"Words from me and my wolf who is tame,
Breathe life into this brightly burning candle flame.
To link (your dog's name) to me walking our life's way,
By a golden thread of love weaving night to link each day.
For my dog to walk, talk, have fun, and in nature to run free
Living happily in trusting, loving harmony with me."

Sprinkle a few drops of ylang-ylang oil into the melted wax around the candle flame. In the candle flame, burn the paper bearing your dog's and your name. Drop the piece of paper into the saucer or dish to burn to ash. Sit stroking and talking to your dog, and give your dog at least one kiss before blowing the candle out.

 Cancer

- **June 22–July 22**
- **Key phrase: I feel for you and need to feel you.**
- **Stones or collar and lead colors: Moonstone, pearl; silver, white.**

Your dog has a genuinely strong sense of self-worth and mission. Their feelings for you run very deep. Your dog's insight and understanding of you could have an inspiring impact. Your dog is especially successful at being a hearing, guiding, therapy, or support dog. Your dog is in touch with your subconscious, theirs, and the supernatural. Around a full moon, your dog will be more psychic and energetic than at other times.

Your dog's foreknowledge will lead you to new people and events that you and they enjoy. They are friendly towards strangers because of their happy home and social life.

Your dog knows how to convince others of its value to do their bidding. A loving home and your constant companionship are very important to your good-looking dog, whose feelings are easily hurt. Your dog can read your facial expressions and can criticize themselves far better than you, so they do not need to be told off, just understood. When traveling, they like the security of having a blanket or toy or sweater of yours from home with them.

Your dog likes outdoor activities, especially where they can take a splash or have a drink out of a tap or bottle. They will not mind a bath, nor will they insist on being in charge of other pets or having the top-dog spot in the home. You are the devoted object of your persuasive dog's affections, and part of their charm is their eye contact. You are their world.

Bonding Spell for You and Your Cancerian Dog Best Friend

Your dog is ruled by the Moon, which rules Monday and the spell ingredients. Monday is a good dog walking and spell-casting day.

You will need:
- A white or silver candle
- A bowl of water
- A hand mirror
- A bunch of roses
- A few pinches of finely ground sea salt in a dish

Take your dog for a waterside walk and let your dog take a splash or have a drink, or lead your dog through a churchyard to have a drink from the water tap.

Place the bowl of water in front of the roses and candle, then light the candle. If it is a moonlit night, hold a hand-mirror up to reflect the Moon. Whether it is a moonlit night or not, hold the mirror over the bowl of water. Stroke your dog's fur with the mirror and show them their face in the mirror. When your dog turns away from the mirror, hold the mirror to reflect the candle flame. Put the mirror down, drop a few pinches of salt into the candle flame, and say:

"From the water reflect the light,
To shine on me and my dog tonight.
(Your dog's name) and I reciprocate our love,
And ask for it to be blessed by heaven above.

> *When the flame flickers and turns,*
> *And the melting wick slowly burns,*
> *I speak into the sacred flame*
> *(Your dog's name) and I go by the same name."*

Draw close to the candle. Into the flame, gently speak your name, followed by your dog's name. Next, speak your dog's name, followed by your name. Ask your dog to bark or be vocal.

Offer your dog the water in the bowl used in the spell. Give your special dog a big fuss while the candle burns. Blow the candles out and take your dog to lie on your bed with you.

 Scorpio

- **October 24–November 21**
- **Key phrase: I live to serve you.**
- **Stones or collar and lead colors: Bloodstone, tourmaline; burgundy.**

Your intuitively obedient, lovable, loyal Scorpio dog attracts other dogs and people like a magnet by approaching them as a friend. Highly emotional with enormous energy and will, your dog needs plenty of exercise and active social interest. They have a great sense for adventure, but beware—they also have the confidence to risk danger, so watch where their nose leads them.

Love inspires their ambition for accomplishment, not force. Being told off deeply hurts your sensitive Scorpio.

Know Your Dog by Their Astrological Sign

You have an excellent, strong-willed working or caring dog who loves water, is fearless of noise, and devotedly protective of children and family pets. Although they are not finicky about food and feeding time, your dog deserves the (affordable) best and a doggy appreciation bag, brought home often.

Your dog enjoys hiding chews and toys and may be jealous of other creatures you show attention or affection to. You have a loyal one-person dog whose mission is to be there for you through thick and thin. You are the most important person in your particularly loving, possessive Scorpio dog's life. There is nothing within their capabilities your dog would not do for you. In return, there is no such thing as too much love from you.

Bonding Spell for You and Your Scorpio Dog Best Friend

Pluto rules your dog, Tuesday, and the spell ingredients, making Tuesday a good dog-walking and spell-casting day.

You will need:
- **A votive candle or a red candle**
- **Dried basil**
- **A small dish**
- **Almond oil**

Pour a couple of teaspoons of basil into a small dish. Sprinkle a few drops of almond oil onto the candle, then roll the candle in the basil, to coat the

candle. If you are using a votive candle, sprinkle droplets of oil on to the top of the candle, followed by a few pinches of basil. Light the candle and say:

> *"As I sprinkle basil onto the candle or into the dish*
> *I begin my wish,*
> *For the spell I've begun,*
> *To bless my dog and I as one.*
> *Flame burn bright, flicker rise and fall,*
> *To light the life, of the best dog of them all."*

Play with or stroke your dog in the candlelight. When the candle is extinguished, sleep with your dog on your bed that night. Or make sure your dog is comfortably settled in their bed with a goodnight kiss.

Chapter Eight

What Your Dog Says About You

𝒴our choice of dog says something about you because a dog is an extension of their owner. Once you become bonded with your dog, you will find that you and your dog not only look alike but that you behave like one another. Your dog's personality becomes like your own, and their behavior will merge with yours.

Your dog copies you because you are the leader of the pack. Your heart must rule the way you treat your dog for your dog to be able to communicate deeply with you. You and your dog will understand one another so well that a look in your eyes will tell your dog what you are thinking or wanting them to do. And if your dog should ever get injured or feel ill, your dog will be able to communicate to you, by sound or a look in their eyes, which part of their body hurts when you touch it, or which part of them feels unwell. A "kiss to make it better" really does help your dog to feel better because it shows them

you have understood they need care for their condition and may need to be seen by a vet.

How you treat your dog encourages their confidence, skills, talents, and traits inherent to their breed to develop, even if your dog is not working at what they were bred to do. For instance, to gather them up, a sheep dog may circularly run around your children, or you in a dog park. Your dog's bred skills may enhance yours.

Gun Dog Group

Including: Pointers, Spaniels, Setters, Retrievers, and the Weimaraner, who help to find, drive, and retrieve game.

Being sociable, you like a lot of varied company around you. You can communicate with people from all walks of life. You are sporting and humorous, hardy and optimistic, and look upon challenges as something to enjoy. You are straightforward, honest, encouraging, active, and always see the best in a person or predicament. You have good manners and say what you think and how you feel. You are clear-minded, affectionate, versatile, and alert to what you hear. You are not critical of what you see. You like music. You are extremely mentally strong and never allow physical problems to mar your happiness. You enjoy walking your dog and being out in the fresh air. You have an enormous amount of energy.

Witty, lovable, imaginative, industrious, inventive, and sincere, you attract a large social circle. Your strength and practical ability to deal with anything in life inspires people you know to be stronger, see things more clearly, and

enjoy life more. You are a cheery optimist who amuses others and gets on with almost everyone, and will never desert a friend. You are impulsive with plenty of ideas, generous and kind. The drive to achieve your small and large goals makes you physically and mentally active. You love simplicity. You are alert to signs you see or hear and are able to realize your future by the indications pointing you in the right direction on your path of good destiny.

Hound Group

Including: Basset Hound, Dachshund, Foxhound, Wolfhound, Deerhound, Saluki, Whippet, Bloodhound, and the Greyhound, who work on scent and sight.

You are a lovable breath of fresh air. By listening to others, you lighten the burden of people's problems. You are sympathetic and advise with a sense of humor. Being good-natured, polite, charming, and unassuming, you do not judge; you help unconditionally.

Alert to opportunities, you take quick action and keep abreast of the times. Because you are cheerful, affectionate, and a good example to other people, they become inspired to emulate your numerous strengths. You see matters through to completion and are determined and driven to achieve your aims because you possess great perseverance and patience. Intuitive, you know what is going to happen in advance because like a hound, you sense what is not yet within sight or hearing.

Being very alert, deep, and analytical, you like to understand life, the meaning of situations and what makes a person tick. Because of your own investigative

nature, you are good at solving your own and other people's concerns. Possessing a strong will, and patience, you are good at putting things right.

A peacemaker, you appreciate beauty and tranquil surroundings, especially liking being out in nature, and may have a strong sense of religion or spirituality. A deep thinker who is very sympathetic, unselfish, kind, and loving, you are tactful in fragile situations. Very clever and empathetic, you may have a much happier life than others.

Terrier Group

Including: Airedale Terrier, Bull Terrier, Cairn Terrier, Fox Terrier, Irish Terrier Australian Terrier, Scottish Terrier, Skye Terrier, Staffordshire Bull Terrier, West Highland White Terrier, and Dandie Dinmont Terrier, which are small vermin killers bred to pursue rodents, badgers, and foxes, and are able to pursue their prey when isolated.

You are high-spirited, cuddly, and may be diminutive in stature but know inside that you are a mighty wolf when challenged. You surprise others with your strength and adaptability. You can be snappy when others are not as fast-thinking as you.

Enterprising, versatile, and someone who puts others first, you are stubborn and independent, patient, energetic, and likeable, well-deserving of love and appreciation. Companionable and hardy, you are resilient to illness and accidents. You possess many talents that you put to good use. Being high spirited, loyal and well-balanced, you dislike confrontations and prefer a gentle approach.

Self-assured and passionate about your beliefs, you avoid putting effort into unworthy causes. Always busy and alert, you rarely simply do nothing because you like to be on the go. You never give up when you have a project to pursue. You are like a dog with a bone when you get your teeth into something. You are driven to seek out excitement and adventure. Multifaceted and adaptable, you are happy in busy company as well as when you are alone, always putting your time to good use and making the most of situations. You are original, creative, and emotional, and stick up for the underdog. You appreciate luxury and thrive when working hard to enjoy expensive things or precious time spent with loved ones.

Toy Group

Toy groups are small, easily manageable dogs, some with no working duties, such as Pekinese, Maltese, King Charles Cavalier-Spaniel, and other historically high-status symbols of royalty and wealth. The Toy Group also includes: Yorkshire Terrier, Pug, Brussels Griffon, English Toy Terrier, Pomeranian, Australian Silky Terrier, Bichon Frise, Italian Greyhound, Papillon, Chinese Crested, and miniature Pinscher.

You are home-loving, authoritarian, exuberant, curious, and speak your mind. You may look timid and vulnerable, but you have an inner strength that shocks those who attempt to take advantage of you. You are analytical and intuitively sensitive, seeing what is hidden and noticing things that are not evident to other people. You have and use your common sense. You are deep and lovable, generous with your time and money and very interesting to know.

Because you do not like hardship, you always find a way to overcome obstacles. Like the Working Group, you possess a rare quality: to be able to turn misfortune into good fortune, because you are very strong and optimistic. People gravitate toward you because you make them feel happier and more able to cope with their own dilemmas.

You have a busy lifestyle and appreciate simplicity and independence. Having a lively mind, you are physically energetic too. Striving for high ideals, you put a lot of effort into achieving the very best that you can for yourself and others. You are versatile and accommodating. You set high goals for yourself and push yourself to the limit, but toward other people, you are more easy-going and less of a taskmaster. You are a good specialist in your chosen field. You have a distinct personality that others warm to easily.

The Utility Group

The Utility dogs were bred for looks and tasks, but their jobs are redundant today. The Dalmatian was bred to run alongside its master's coach and horses. The Lhasa Apso was bred to alarm intruders of the Dalai Lama's Palace. The Utility Group also includes Bulldog, Chow-Chow, Herman Spitz, Mexican hairless dog, Tibetan Spaniel, Tibetan Terrier, and Toy, Miniature, and Standard Poodles.

You are very sensitive, clean, neat, need lots of people around you, and fear loneliness. You have a good memory and an alert, creative, imaginative mind. You are talented in the arts. You have a good sense of humor and are

self-confident, conventional, polite, and well-mannered. You like to please and keep everybody happy but can be too accommodating of others to the detriment of yourself. Your sympathetic good nature leaves you open for others to take advantage. Security is important to you. You will not risk asking a favor without feeling sure the person you ask will oblige.

You have great stamina to persevere and patiently see a project through to completion, but you learn quickly and are practical, because you dislike drudgery. You are inventive, strong-willed, and quick-thinking, but also philosophical. You attract very unusual opportunities which present themselves to you. You enjoy travel, especially long-distance. You have a strong desire to get your own way and have a talent for being very well organized, tidy, and trustworthy. You are original and reliable, and probably dress flamboyantly or colorfully. The fun, carefree way you have about you truly cheers and brightens the lives of those you meet.

Working Group

Including: Rottweiler, Siberian Husky, St. Bernard, Pyrenean Mastiff, Bullmastiff, Great Dane, Giant Schnauzer, German Pinscher, Canadian Eskimo Dog, Boxer, Dobermann, and Newfoundland, all bred for tasks that help humankind to labor.

You are self-disciplined, good-natured, like life outdoors, and are cheerful, confident, courageous, and a good organizer. You can withstand difficulties and, by your kindness, win over hardship because of your perseverance and belief in what is right and good. You look after your nearest and dearest, as well as sentimental items. You love meeting new people, exploring unfamiliar situations, and traveling to interesting places. You are fearlessly good at sports, thriving on challenges and unique experiences that satisfy your physical stamina and fulfill your peace of mind. You are mentally and physically strong. Purposeful and focused, you put a lot of effort in to succeed.

You can be stubborn and inactive when you feel disrespected or unappreciated. You thrive on praise and falter on criticism. Your bark can be bigger than your bite when someone upsets you, and you always stand your ground. You have many splendid qualities you use to help others. Similar to the Toy Group, your optimistic way of looking at situations gives you a rare ability to turn either your own or other peoples' misfortune into good fortune. You have a flair for good taste that you like to display in your home décor, style of clothes, or in a distinctive hobby or art. At home, you are a perfect and entertaining hostess. You are as faithful to your friends as your dog is to you and can be relied upon to help, when help is needed. You look upon people kindly and do your best to keep everybody happy.

Pastoral Group

Including: Australian Cattle dog, Belgian Shepherd, Border Collie, Komondor, Old English Sheepdog, Welsh Corgi, Marema Sheepdog, German Shepherd, and Briard, all bred to help people with flocks and herds.

You are quick to learn and use your initiative. Liking work, you are stable, can concentrate for long periods, and are not easily distracted. Confident and

tolerant of other people's mistakes, you are reserved and gentle with others, more forgiving of them than you are of yourself, and a very good leader and peacemaker. You are a very adaptable, spiritual person with a wide network of friends. Some are unusual people or live in rare places, attracted to you because you are comfortable being yourself. Totally focused on achieving your goal, and tireless in your ambition to succeed in whatever you set your mind on; you do not rest. You are self-reliant and independent, considerate of others and help them the best that you can. A peacemaker, you always try to smooth things over with quarrelsome people. Your sense of purpose makes you a leader rather than a follower. Clever, inventive, and skilled, you put special talents that you possess to very good use. You are a good organizer who enjoys, by some focal point, bringing other people together socially. You enjoy change and will travel long distances, but prefer to take a holiday where your dog can accompany you. You thrive on entertainment and like music and the arts. You have a natural gift for communicating with animals. You are fun to know, living your life with a great sense of humor and faith in good destiny prevailing.

Mongrels

Mongrels generally live longer than pedigree dogs. Mongrels have fewer physical defects, are more resilient to illness, and are usually non-aggressive and less neurotic.

You probably love being kind to everyone, spoiling your dog, and living in a very strong family environment. You may be very posh, but you are not a snob. You like to be straightforward with people and appreciate those who are honest in return. You are efficient, well-organized, and good at prioritizing and multitasking. You are practical, caring, encouraging, and sympathetic. You help people who are the underdogs or who don't see themselves as the perfect specimen that they wish they were. You take on other people's problems, deal with them for them, and teach them how to manage their predicaments for the future. You have an ability to see into a person's soul and discover their true ideals, wishes, feelings, and sentiments. You enhance other people's lives and give them the confidence to be happy and secure in the knowledge that they are more powerful than they realize. You cultivate your own—and their—psychic abilities to walk life's path that is right for you or them.

Being quick and thorough in your tasks, you may be inclined to overwork yourself because you have a strong sense of duty and moral obligation. You attract a lot of social success because you easily make a lot of friends. You possess good qualities inherited from your mother. Your strong emotions mean you may easily react to different environments. You are domesticated, love home, companionship, and home comforts, but also enjoy excitement, adventure and taking great leaps of faith into the unknown.

Using the Dog Oracle

Decide which one of the ten methods of consulting the Dog Oracle you will use for your dog to divine the answer to your question. Then, choose a question from the list of Dog Oracle questions on the next page.

Sixteen Dog Oracle Questions

1. Will (name of person) be as faithful as my dog is to me?
3. Is this relationship wise?
5. Will my plans be successful?
7. Will (name of person) contact me again?
9. Will the matter I have in mind turn out happily for me?
11. Will I be rich?
13. Will I be popular?
15. Will I attract a wonderful, loving partner?
17. Will I move to another part of the country?
19. Does God exist?
21. Will I avoid misfortune?
23. Will I travel around the world?
25. Will I have my own home?
27. Will I have a family?
29. Who is the one destined to be my partner?
31. Do I have a Guardian Angel?

Methods to Consult the Dog Oracle

Method One: The Tail-Wagging Fun Way

Choose a question from the list of sixteen questions and remember the question number. Hold the Dog Oracle chart of sixteen dog symbols on pages 140-141 so your dog can touch one of the squares with the tip of their tail when you speak the question aloud to them.

The square your dog touches with the tip of their tail is the symbol you must find at the top of the chart that has sixteen dogs at the top and question numbers running down.

You will find the page number to turn to, answering your question, by finding your question number running down the left-hand-side of the chart. Trace your finger down from the dog symbol that is the same as the one your dog's tail touched. From your question number, trace your left finger to the right until both fingers meet on one square that contains a symbol. Turn to the page headed by that symbol. Your answer will be beside the dog symbol your dog's tail touched when you spoke your question aloud and held the chart of sixteen dogs to your dog to wag their tail on.

Method Two: Shake a Paw with a Coin Divination

Sit beside your dog so that your bodies touch. Remember your question number. Hold a coin in your hand. Hold your dog's paw in the same hand

and speak your question aloud while you shake the coin and throw it on to the chart of sixteen dog symbols. Remember which dog symbol the coin fell onto.

Refer to the chart by looking at your question number in the left-hand column running down the chart. At the top of that same page, find the dog symbol your coin landed on. Trace your finger down from the dog symbol to a square that meets your question number's line when you trace your left forefinger from your question number towards the right. The square your fingers meet on will give you a symbol. That symbol is the page number to turn to for the answer to your question. On the page number you are told to turn to, you will find your answer beside the same symbol the coin landed on.

Method Three: Please Give Me Your Paw Divination

Choose a question and remember the question number. To get your dog to touch a square with their paw, sit them in front of the chart. Place the chart on the floor or hold the chart up to your dog. Ask your dog your question and say: *"(Name of dog), please give me your paw."* Notice which of the sixteen dog symbols your dog's paw touches.

Look for that same dog symbol in the line at the top of the chart. Running down the left-hand side of the page, find your question number and, using your index finger, trace a line from your question number until it meets a square that your finger can trace up to the symbol at the top of the chart that your dog pointed their paw at when you held the chart and spoke your question to them.

Using the Dog Oracle

The square where these two symbols meet will give you a symbol. That symbol is the page to turn to for your answer. Your answer will be beside the same symbol your dog touched with their paw.

Method Four: Dog Biscuit and Kiss Divination

Choose a question from the list and remember your question number. Call your dog to accompany you while you take a biscuit from their dish, or biscuit box. Sit comfortably with your dog and place the chart of sixteen dog symbols on the floor in front of you. Close your eyes, kiss your dog on the head while you hold the biscuit in your hand, and ask your question aloud to your dog. Kiss your dog again, close your eyes, and say *"I love you"* to your dog, while you throw the biscuit onto the chart of sixteen symbols.

Remember the dog symbol and your question number. Turn the book pages to find the dog symbol heading the chart and your question number in the left-hand column of the chart. Trace your finger along from your question number to a square that meets where you trace your finger down from the symbol the dog biscuit landed on. That square will give you a symbol heading page. Turn to that page. Your answer will be found beside the same symbol your dog's biscuit landed on.

Give your dog the biscuit to eat for being such a clever dog, and read the Dog Oracle answer your special dog led you to.

Method Five: Please Catch the Dog Biscuit and Fetch the Dog Prophecy to Me

From the list of questions, choose a question and remember the question number. Place the chart of sixteen dog symbols on the floor. Speak your question aloud to your dog. Throw a biscuit to your dog and ask them to drop the biscuit on one of the sixteen dog symbols on the page. Tell your dog what a clever, wise, and insightful special dog they are to have dropped that biscuit on that symbol.

Remember the symbol that your dog dropped the biscuit on. Turn to the chart and find your question number in the left-hand column running down the page. Running across the top of the chart, find the same dog symbol that your dog dropped the biscuit on. Trace your finger down from the dog symbol until it meets a square on the same line as your question number, when you trace from left to right. The symbol in that square will tell you which page to turn to for your answer. On that page, your answer will be beside the same symbol that your dog dropped the biscuit on. Give your dog the biscuit to eat while you read your Good Dog Oracle answer.

Method Six: The Shake the Coin from Furry Paw Prophecy

Choose a question and remember the question number. Sit beside your dog and place the chart of sixteen symbols in front of you both. Kiss your dog's paw, then place a coin on top of your dog's paw and continue to hold it. Ask your question aloud and lift your dog's paw to toss the coin onto the sixteen dog symbols chart.

Remember which symbol the coin landed on, then turn to the chart. Find your question number running down the left-hand-side of the chart. Trace your finger across the chart until it meets a square that also traces down the chart, from the symbol that the coin landed on. The square that meets gives you a symbol heading a page that tells you what page to turn to for your answer. Your answer will be beside the same symbol the coin landed on from your furry friend's paw.

Method Seven: My Sniffer-Dog Divination

Choose a question from the list and remember your question number. Sit with your dog beside you and the chart of sixteen dog symbols in front of you. Close your eyes and cuddle your dog while you speak your question aloud to your dog. Tell your dog that you want them to touch or sniff a symbol with their nose. Keeping your eyes closed, point at the sixteen dogs chart for your dog to touch or sniff. Open your eyes quickly to see which of the sixteen dog symbols your dog sniffed or touched with their nose.

Turn to the chart, find the number of your question in the left-hand column. With your forefinger, trace straight from it toward the right until you reach the column headed with the dog symbol your dog sniffed or touched with their nose. Trace down from the top symbol until it meets a square on the same line as your question number. The symbol in the meeting square is the page headed by that symbol to turn to for your answer. Your answer will be beside the same symbol your dog sniffed or touched with their nose.

Method Eight: Little Dog Divination

If you have a little dog, you could let your dog walk on the chart of sixteen symbols, making a note of which symbol your dog walks on first. Alternatively, you could take your dog's paw-print on a piece of card. Cut around the paw-print. Drop the paw-print onto the board to see which of the sixteen symbols the paw-print falls on.

Either way, remember your question number and turn to the chart. Find your question number in the left-hand column. Trace from your question number, toward the right until you reach the column headed by the same symbol your dog touched with their paw. The symbol in the square where across and down meet is the page headed by that symbol to turn to for the Good Dog Oracle answer. Your answer will be beside the symbol your dog walked on or paw-print fell on.

Method Nine: Your Dog's Collar or Lead Dowsing Divination

Choose your question number from the list of questions on page 130. Sit with your dog and place the chart of sixteen dog symbols on the floor in front of you both.

Remove your dog's collar from their neck or where you keep it indoors. Wind your dog's collar around your forefinger so that your dog's nametag and the heavy end of your dog's collar is suspended by your forefinger, an inch or two above the chart of sixteen dog symbols. Swing the collar in one clockwise circle. Close your eyes and, with your other hand, stroke your dog from the top of their

head to the end of their back, the same number of times the number of your question. Question 13, for example, would mean your dog gets thirteen strokes.

When your dog's collar has stopped swinging, open your eyes and look at the symbol on the square that your dog's collar is suspended above.

Alternatively, hold your dog's collar in the palm of your hand and suspend the nametag between your forefinger and middle finger. Close your eyes and move the back of your hand over the chart. Open your eyes to see which of the symbols the name is suspended above. If you prefer not to remove your dog's collar, you could instead suspend the clip end of your dog's lead between your forefinger and middle finger.

Look at the chart to find your question number in the left-hand column running down the page. In the row running across the top of the page, find the same symbol that your dog's nametag or lead halted above. Trace your right forefinger down to meet a square that coincides with your question number when you trace left. The symbol in the square that meets both is the page headed by that symbol to turn to for your answer. Your answer will be beside the symbol your dog's nametag or lead settled still above.

Method Ten: Your Good Dog's Mathematical Divination

Choose a question number and remember it. Look at the chart of sixteen dog symbols and place four dog biscuits in four rows, or four dog treats in four rows in the shape of the sixteen dog symbols chart.

Show your dog the biscuits or treats laid out in the shape of the chart so that your dog will pick up one of the sixteen in their mouth. The numerical biscuit your dog chooses is the one that relates to the symbol in the spot on the chart. Note which symbol the biscuit replaces and go to that symbol at the top of the chart. Trace your finger down from the symbol to a square that meets your question number when traced from the left. The symbol in the square where tracing down and left, meet, gives you the page headed by that symbol to turn to for your Good Dog Oracle answer.

Your answer on that page will be beside the symbol the dog-biscuit or treat, represented in the sixteen dog symbols chart.

The Good Dog Spell Book

Using the Dog Oracle

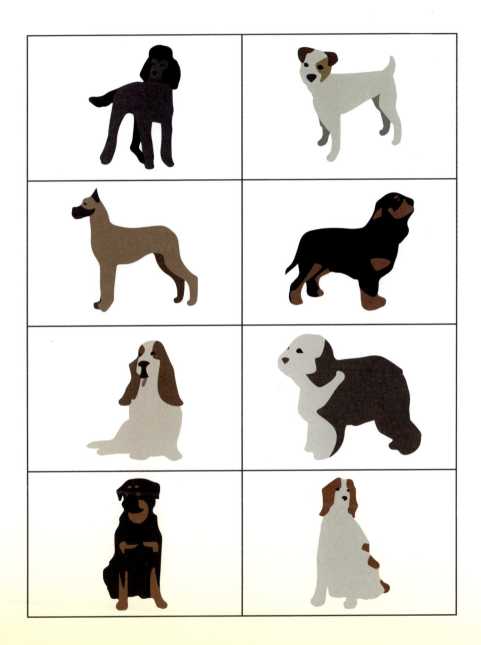

The Good Dog Spell Book

	Yes, the one you are asking about will. Be patient for a little longer.
	Yes, you will, sooner than anticipated and it will be a lovely one that you will enjoy very much.
	They are destined to be. You have all the ingredients for success within you. Believe in yourself.
	Yes, if you keep your wits about you and do not allow yourself to get sidetracked.
	A very good one is with you your whole life, from birth to death.
	You have nothing at all to fear because you are sensible and intuitive in all that you do.
	In nature and in you. You will encounter a providential occurrence.
	One who has a good sense of humor, fine physique, and is attractive to you.
	Destiny is at work. You will feel cared for and safe with one before the end of this year.
	Yes, you will be by your own determination and in more ways than one definition.
	No, the person you are asking about will not. But they still will be.
	Yes, you can expect that you will because you choose to.
	You will get the chance to alone, with other people and with someone special too.
	It will make you happy for a while but, by your choice, may not last forevermore.
	You already are. The proof is there that you are in high demand.
	Yes, a very loving, strong one to be proud of.

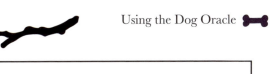

Using the Dog Oracle

	Yes, you will feel happy and it will end happily.
	You will not suffer any harm. Fear is a pessimist, faith is an optimist.
	One who will surprisingly not look like you expect.
	With respected people who matter, especially yes.
	Yes, and it will grow quite large and be admired.
	The person will ask you to meet them. You are on their mind more than you realize.
	Their mission is to look after you in every way every day. Ask for a sign—you'll get one.
	Quite soon and more than one, but not necessarily more than one at the same time.
	Yes, it is light in your dog, nature, and you. Proof will be given by asking.
	Reasonably, yes. You will not suffer hardship.
	You will benefit enormously.
	Not too far away and to your liking.
	The one you are asking about would like you to think so. Your dog wins.
	You will be spoiled for choice. In time, you most certainly will.
	Yes, your whole life long.
	Undoubtedly. Of course they will. Keep heading for your goal and what you know is right.

The Good Dog Spell Book

	Certainly, yes. Within the next twelve months.
	You will receive an invitation very soon.
	Yes. More than you realize.
	Yes, because you are putting your heart and soul into it.
	One special one always, and some when the according to your needs.
	You will live a charmed, lucky existence. You play by the rules.
	Yes, when the time feels right. It will be light, bright and sunny.
	Yes. It is light and energy in every living thing. Supernatural events will occur for you.
	The one you are asking about intends to be. It has a tough component to match.
	Have peace of mind. You really should not doubt that it will. Your fears are unfounded.
	It is entirely up to you. Someone will ask you to, but you may decline the offer.
	Through your own efforts and good fortune, you will.
	A harmonious, happy one that is fun.
	Only until you see through the agenda of the one in question. Be alert like your dog.
	One close to your home.
	The opportunity for you to will arrive quite soon.

Using the Dog Oracle

	Yes, and one that is always there for you in times of need and uncertainty.
	Yes, and idyllic for you.
	If you ask to see them, they will appear to you in your mind's eye.
	You really have no reason to be anxious. They will at the right time for you, you see.
	It is the life force of love and light. You already know it in your heart.
	Yes, where other people you know never will.
	You really should not doubt that it will.
	One you meet by a happy twist of fate.
	Certainly, by your very nature, yes.
	Yes, very, in many more ways than one.
	Not quite, because they are unable to spend as much time with you as the top dog.
	It may not last for long because you have a change of heart.
	Very, without a doubt. You are kind and a good listener.
	Yes, you have a genuine purpose for them to be.
	Yes, your conscience is your guide. You are safe.
	One that feels so pleasant that people remark upon it.

The Good Dog Spell Book

	To prove yes, ask them to help with a personal dilemma. You will see the situation improve.
	When they want to, then they will.
	Yes, through your own desire.
	A friendly one with many visitors.
	A close and strong ally to you. You will experience great happiness.
	You already know, deep inside yourself, that the answer is yes.
	Your magnetism captivates many but particularly one.
	Because you are sensible and think before you ask or act, yes.
	Yes, your heart tells you so. Keep looking forward.
	Yes, and emotionally too.
	Yes, more than once if that is what you would like.
	There is no competition. Paws up wins.
	It will help you to feel inspired for a while, but not always and forever.
	You will meet where music plays.
	It will and time works to your advantage.
	You most certainly are and always will be.

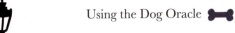

	Both like to sleep with you, but the furriest one is the winner.
	You will, but a battle of will might ensue first.
	Helping you to make the right decisions every day, because they love you.
	Very comfortable with luxuries and a pleasant lifestyle.
	Your paths will cross through a shared interest.
	That is something you can be sure of.
	You and others want it for you. Yes.
	Yes, but they may take a little longer than you had thought they would.
	Yes, for both of you it is.
	Your magnetism captivates a special someone near water.
	Yes, when you can afford to and want to.
	To many interesting, unusual locations.
	Without a doubt, working through your life whether you realize it or not.
	Where there is a will, there is a way. They could if they wanted to. They will.
	You will, undoubtedly yes.
	With certainty.

The Good Dog Spell Book

	You like the sound of their voice and humor.
	Yes, and it will be pleasurable.
	A lot more than other people you mix with.
	That's how miracles have happened and will happen for you. Rest assured.
	Yes, it will be somewhere you have not yet been to.
	Keep believing in them, yes.
	You cannot please all people all of the time. Mostly yes.
	An intelligent, gifted, and warm, strong one.
	It is their intention. They do what they say.
	It will be adventurous.
	They will find you. Fate has ordained it.
	Yes, because you are receptive to good advice.
	You will if you want to and put effort in.
	Quite easily, because you abide in your destiny by being wisely superior to fate.
	Nothing can live without the four elements of Earth, Air, Fire, and Water. Yes.
	In the fullness of time, yes.

Using the Dog Oracle

	Yes, of course, without a doubt. You will.
	Yes, and very suitably, if things carry on the way they are.
	You are destined to before too long.
	You will because you are well organized and possess great wisdom.
	Yes, with news and an offer.
	They are aware of everything you are experiencing now as well as during your future.
	You will simply because you would like to.
	Yes, because you find it rewarding fun and great entertainment.
	You may dream of their appearance just before a well-destined meeting occurs.
	It cannot be prevented. Of course.
	It is one that has the potential to be long-lasting.
	Yes, but initially it will take a little perseverance and time.
	Yes, but not quite as efficiently.
	Yes, but not consistently if you are foolish when good fortune comes your way.
	Yes, the result will be as you wish.
	Invite them to prove yes to you and they will confirm their affection for you.

The Good Dog Spell Book

	Yes, a large one.
	Yes, and very much to your liking.
	Someone who considers and puts you first.
	You will, and any minor you will always turn to good fortune.
	To near and far with enjoyment.
	Through wonders in your good dog, you, and other people.
	One where your heart is.
	One who works with you and helps you in every way that they can, especially when you ask.
	A premonition dream or a daytime sign recognized by you reveals great personal success.
	Yes, when you least expect it to happen.
	It is well-deserved, yes. There is no reason why not.
	Your wish will be granted. Enjoy watching it unfold.
	Yes, you won't have to wait too long.
	Yes, through something good that brings you peace of mind.
	If it is based on true, genuine love, yes.
	Yes, if their love is unconditional.

Using the Dog Oracle

	If you are organized and persevere, yes.
	Have no fear of course you will. It occurs naturally.
	Yes you will, consistently.
	One who has made happy things happen for you that you would call "good luck."
	By your own skill and intelligence, yes.
	What delays them is that they know you deserve better.
	It will not seek you, so yes, do not worry. All will go well.
	A visionary who has great insight into people and situations.
	If you are at the top of their list of priorities, yes.
	With great certainty you can be assured, yes.
	By being in the right place at the right time with the right people.
	To more than one other, you will, yes.
	Yes, a very good one.
	Yes, you would freeze or starve if not. All the signs are there telling you yes.
	Through your own industrious effort, invention, and versatility.
	They have high standards to live up to and do their best.

The Good Dog Spell Book

	Yes, and it will be very desirable.
	Yes. Feel safe in the knowledge that you will.
	Because you are careful about not taking risky chances, yes.
	Yes, for a pleasant reason.
	Within your heart, you feel and know it is within and working through you.
	Good looking, reasonably rich, hard-working, and great fun.
	People will ask you to and you will.
	Do not entertain thoughts of doubt. You are right to think positively.
	One that others are fond of and want to know.
	They will. Your future looks brighter as a result.
	Yes, expect good news quite soon.
	Yes, even though they do not have the same amount of time in your company.
	It cannot be prevented; without purposely trying, you will make yourself.
	As long as you remember people can tell you anything. So, really, no.
	You will build a personal friendship if you work with them and ask for help.
	You will. You are destined to. Love will always find a way.

Using the Dog Oracle

	They will admire and help you, and you will recognize them for their importance.
	Yes, surrounded by friends and family.
	You will. Yes.
	You wish to and will. It is your preordained destiny.
	Yes, ask them to let you know who they are, and you will get to know them. The more you thank them the more they give you.
	Yes. Because you are much more prudent in the future than at present.
	Yes. Your sense that it lightens your darkness is right. Keep believing; excellent things are in store for you.
	Yes, you will, and you will love it.
	Somewhere you have not been to yet.
	If you sense no, you are right. Someone maybe leading you up the garden path and it is not your dog.
	More than one finds you irresistible. You are spoiled for choice.
	You are making it so that it will. Be fearless.
	With many, and it will escalate your whole life long.
	Your intuition tells you yes, so do not doubt. Success is certain.
	There seems to be too much entanglement for it to be at the moment. It could be in the future.
	Yes, but you would be wise not to entertain a fool.

The Good Dog Spell Book

	Yes. Intuitively you knew. That is the reason why you commenced them. Keep forging ahead.
	One you love that loves you very much. It will be a very happy one.
	A great one, especially for entertaining.
	A lot, and a lot more, if that is what you would like to do.
	You are far luckier than many others. Justice is on your side.
	When you are a little older and wiser you will. And you will know it in your heart when you do.
	Yes. Trust and you will feel better.
	A giver, not a taker, who does what they do for you because they love you.
	You have worked so hard for it to, so it will. It is right that it should.
	They nudge the jigsaw pieces of your life into place so all goes well. They deserve your recognition.
	You will decide to and will be happy.
	Not quite as well trained as your dog. But they could be.
	With all sorts of people from all walks of life.
	At their convenience when they have something to gain.
	For a short time, not a long time. You will decide when that is.
	By your talent and partnership.

Using the Dog Oracle

	A happy and fun one with the right person, yes.
	It is their mission to assist you in everything you do. Make it easier for them and you make it easier for you too.
	You will, a lot. Many adventures are waiting to be explored.
	You will find it is right for you to.
	Yes. Hope and believe something wonderful will happen, it will.
	Eventually, but not soon. What you aim for you get. Don't take risks.
	They would have by now had they wanted to.
	You most certainly will.
	Not quite, but almost as. The competition is fierce.
	Yes, it will bring happiness.
	Quite easily, because you are self-composed.
	With many important people, yes.
	The prediction is they will.
	Yes, if you take positive action and use your initiative.
	They honor words by commitment and deeds.
	It will happen in the spring or summer.

🦴 The Good Dog Spell Book

	You will know it the first time you meet.
	Yes. But you are not desperate and so should not easily fall in with their plans.
	Absolutely yes. Without fail it cannot be prevented.
	Keep believing, yes.
	Yes, you will.
	A very personal, interesting one.
	If you would like to, because numerous opportunities will arrive.
	Yes, you are very able.
	Quite soon you will. You probably already sense yes. You are right to be hopeful.
	Yes, when the time is right, but not yet.
	Yes, because it is in your heart and mind to.
	In one way, yes, but perhaps not for the first reason you think.
	Because of the care you put in, yes. You will be happily surprised.
	The one you are asking about is capable of it.
	By more means than one.
	Ask for their help. It will be given and you will have no doubt.

Using the Dog Oracle

	There will be an instant connection and knowing. It is already written in the stars.
	Yes, if you listen to your own good advice and act accordingly. Have peace of mind.
	Quite soon.
	The person in question will always devotedly help you whenever you ask.
	Everything is in good order. What you want will come through for you.
	Yes, and it is one that will be very well suited to you.
	Yes, with the right person you most certainly will.
	Yes, don't stop believing and never give up.
	One you can thank for keeping harm at bay and for bringing you little and big miracles.
	The answer is yes. It is you who will make it happen.
	You already expect you will, because you know you will. Your sixth sense is strong.
	Yes, with all except those who are jealous.
	Very happily, and with little fuss.
	Yes, because you have every good reason to feel confident.
	If you are astute, you will learn a great deal from it.
	Obstacles prevent it for some time. Meanwhile, move on. Something much happier is forecasted for you.

157

Index

A

Agate, 99
Air, 35–36, 43, 61, 99, 101, 118–119
Almond, 13, 25, 52–53, 57, 101–102, 113
Amber, 87, 94
Amethyst, 104
Animal, 2–3, 5, 102, 125
Ankh, 4
Anubis, 4
Apricot, 103–104
April, 85, 92
Apso, 122
Aquamarine, 107
Aquarius, 99, 104, 106
Aries, 84–86
Ash, 12, 19, 51, 87, 109
August, 8, 10, 87, 94

B

Basil, 51, 113–114
Bergamot, 95–96
Bind, 11, 22–23, 83
Bless, 13, 21, 50, 75, 96, 98, 104, 111, 114
Bloodstone, 112
Blue, 27, 35–36, 57, 62, 90, 98, 102, 104, 106–107
Bone, 5, 87, 95, 121
Bury, 5, 9, 12, 19, 28, 30, 32, 36, 39, 45, 76, 81, 87

C

Cancer, 107, 110
Candle, 8–14, 18–28, 30–31, 37–39, 43–46, 48–52, 57–62, 66–67, 76, 86–89, 91, 93–96, 98, 101–104, 106, 108–109, 111–114
Capricorn, 92, 97–99
Cat, 3, 5–6, 65
Cedar, 60
Chamomile, 57
Circle, 12, 31, 48–49, 69, 73, 75, 91, 102–103, 106, 118, 136
Clove, 31, 38–39, 91

Coin, 8–9, 44–45, 48–49, 131–132, 134–135
Communication, 55, 58, 99–100, 108, 117–118
Confidence, 60, 112, 118, 126
Crossroad, 28
Crystal, 22, 58–59, 89

D
Death, 4, 65, 77
December, 90, 97
Diamond, 85
Divination, 14, 65–72, 80, 131–133, 135–137
Dusk, 2, 7, 11, 14, 26–28, 70

E
Earth, 3, 21, 43, 75, 81, 92, 96, 98
Emerald, 92, 99
Eucalyptus, 51–52, 60

F
Familiar, 1, 6, 8, 10–11, 23, 59, 83
February, 104, 107
Fire, 3, 43, 52, 84–85, 90
Flame, 10, 12–13, 18–19, 22, 24, 26–28, 38–39, 49, 51–52, 57–60, 66–67, 76, 87, 89, 94, 96, 98, 102, 104, 109, 111–112, 114
Flower, 11, 13, 43, 99
Fortune, 43, 53, 122, 124
Frankincense, 60
Full Moon, 44, 49–50, 75, 110
Fur, 2, 24, 26, 31, 36, 41, 44, 46–47, 59–61, 67, 76, 78, 88–89, 96, 99, 103–104, 109, 111

G
Garden, 5, 8, 11, 18, 31, 45, 50, 56, 86, 92
Garlic, 31, 38–39
Garnet, 97
Gemini, 99–101
German, 123–124
Ghost, 65–66, 76
Gold, 10, 23, 44, 47–48, 87
Green, 44, 46–48, 50–51, 61, 66, 90, 92–93, 98, 107

H
Halloween, 65
Happiness, 35–36, 75, 83, 87, 98, 118
Healing, 55–56, 59, 62
Heart, 3, 11, 17, 20, 22, 24, 26–27, 30–31, 55, 62, 77, 89, 117

Index

I
Illness, 5, 76, 120, 125

J
Jackal, 4, 6
January, 97, 104
July, 8, 10, 87, 110
June, 11, 99, 110
Jupiter, 91

L
Lavender, 13, 37, 57, 95–96, 101–102
Lemon, 13, 37, 61
Leo, 84, 87–89
Libra, 99, 102–103
Lilac, 57, 104
Lion, 3
Love, 2, 5–7, 9–10, 17, 19–20, 22, 24, 26–28, 30–32, 50, 53, 66–67, 75, 83–85, 87–88, 90–97, 99–100, 103–106, 109, 111–113, 119–120, 124–126, 133
Loyalty, 1–2, 7, 21, 84–86, 99, 101–102, 107–108, 112–113, 120

M
Marjoram, 60
Mercury, 95, 101
Mimosa, 98–99
Mint, 25, 61
Mirror, 1, 8–9, 11–12, 75, 101–102, 111
Money, 6, 39, 44–47, 49–51, 73, 121
Moon, 30–31, 44–45, 48–50, 75, 110–111
Moonstone, 110

N
Neptune, 108
New Moon, 44
Night, 10, 21, 39, 44, 51, 65, 72, 74–75, 78, 109, 111, 114
November, 90, 112
Nutmeg, 61, 108–109

O
Oak, 76, 91
October, 102, 112
Oil, 13–14, 18–19, 25–26, 37, 43, 51–53, 57, 60–62, 88–89, 93–96, 101–104, 109, 113–114
Omens, 65–66, 76–79
Opal, 102
Oracle, 128–131, 133–134, 136, 138
Orange, 10, 61, 87

161

P

Paw, 2, 8–9, 11, 14, 38, 40, 45, 48–49, 52–53, 65, 68, 73, 81, 91–92, 94, 98, 108, 131–136
Peridot, 94
Petal, 11, 18–19, 24, 30, 37, 81
Pink, 11, 18–20, 25–26, 31–32, 94, 102–103
Pisces, 107–108
Plant, 11, 18, 31, 43, 45, 81, 106
Pluto, 113
Protection, 9, 12, 65, 77, 85, 87
Psychic, 2, 9, 110, 126
Purple, 57, 104

Q

Quartz, 22, 26, 58–59, 88–89

R

Red, 10, 20–21, 23–24, 86, 97, 113
Rose, 8–9, 11–12, 18–22, 24, 26, 30–31, 37, 59, 62, 81, 88–89, 93–94, 111
Rosemary, 52–53, 60–61
Ruby, 85, 97

S

Sage, 25, 60, 72
Sagittarius, 84, 90–91
Salt, 8, 24, 38–39, 51–52, 93–94, 101–102, 111
Sandalwood, 25, 88–89
Saturn, 98
Scorpio, 107, 112–113
Sea, 24, 28, 38–40, 43, 51, 111
Security, 49, 108, 110, 123
September, 94, 102
Sleep, 5, 7, 46, 50, 72, 74, 81, 85, 103, 108, 114
Spirit, 1–2, 7, 44, 88, 104–105
Stone, 3, 6, 29, 75, 80, 85, 87, 90, 92, 94, 97, 99, 102, 104, 107, 110, 112
Sun, 8, 10–11, 84, 87–89, 96
Symbol, 4, 37, 121, 131–138

T

Taurus, 92–93
Thyme, 60, 103–104
Tourmaline, 112
Tree, 7, 22, 28–29, 32, 36, 56, 58, 74, 76, 80, 91, 106
Turquoise, 90, 99

U

Uranus, 106

Index

V
Venus, 93, 103
Virgo, 92, 94–95

W
Water, 8, 11, 13–14, 21, 27, 38–40, 43–45, 48–49, 57, 61–62, 69–70, 73, 85, 99, 106–109, 111–113
Waxing Moon, 30–31, 44–45
Wealth, 43–46, 48–50, 73, 75, 121
Weather, 93–94
Whisker, 24, 47
Willow, 76
Wolf, 1–8, 11, 14, 26–28, 44, 70, 109, 120

Y
Yellow, 10, 87–88, 94, 99, 101
Ylang Ylang, 25, 52–53, 57, 60–61, 109